# In Case of Emergency, Break Childhood

## A Gen Xer's Survival Guide to Anxiety, Addiction, and Accidental Enlightenment

### Jason Mayo

SOBER NOT SUBTLE MEDIA

In Case of Emergency, Break Childhood

By Jason Mayo

Copyright © 2025 by Jason Mayo

Published by Sober Not Subtle™, an advocacy platform committed to ending the stigma around addiction and mental health.

Sober Not Subtle™ is a trademark of Jason Mayo.

Professional publishing services rendered by A-Team Press, LLC

amylizharrison.com/a-teampressauthorpublishingservices

This is a work of nonfiction. Names and identifying details may have been changed to protect privacy. The views expressed are those of the author.

Printed in the United States of America

First Edition

# Contents

## Part Three

## I'm Better

*For anyone who grew up believing they were too broken to fix.*

***For my wife****—who stayed when it would've been easier to leave, and saved my life more times than she knows. You're still the one.*

***For my daughters****—thank you for making me laugh, giving me purpose, and keeping my ego in check.*

***For my mom****—who carried the load while I made it heavier. I get it now. Thank you.*

*And thank you to **Playlist #3***—*You were like a weighted blanket for my subconscious while I tried to make sense of it all.*

# Author's Note

This is a true story, told to the best of my recollection—unfortunately, the brain cells I lost along the way didn't leave a paper trail.

To protect the privacy of certain individuals—and because not everyone signed up to be in a book—some names, locations, and identifying details have been changed. A few characters are composites. Some events have been condensed, rearranged, or recreated as accurately as memory allows. And memory? It's not a filing cabinet —it's more like a mood.

Any resemblance to real people beyond those intentionally included is purely coincidental. Unless you're absolutely sure it's you. In that case... maybe call your shrink.

# Preface

I never thought I'd write a book—definitely not one about myself. Most people in their right mind wouldn't want to share the embarrassing stuff, the shameful stuff, the ridiculous, painful, fucked-up shit. But here's the thing: not sharing was exactly what got me here in the first place.

Holding all that in? It chews you up. It rots you from the inside out.

Mental health is real. And it's important that people understand it. Not being able to get out of bed isn't always laziness. Addiction doesn't always look like a junkie passed out under a park bench with a needle in their arm. Sometimes it looks like the guy in the next cubicle. The mom in the carpool. The dude laughing a little too loud at the party.

Sometimes, it's unrecognizable—even to ourselves.

That's why I'm writing this. For awareness. For honesty. To help normalize the conversation we're all dying to have but too scared to start.

When I first got sober, my AA sponsor asked me to write out my drinking history. Most people scribble a page or two. Bullet points. A journal entry. Not me. I wrote fifteen pages, starting with my childhood and ending on the day I put down the bottle and the pills.

We read it together. Then I tucked it away on a hard drive and forgot about it.

Fifteen years later, I was cleaning out a drawer, found the drive, and popped it in. And there it was—like a time capsule from my darkest self. The memories were fuzzy, but the words weren't. It hit me like a punch to the gut. And for some reason, instead of walking away, I kept writing.

It started as therapy. It turned into this.

Every time I sat down to work on it, I cried. No exaggeration. This thing picked open a ton of old scabs. But turns out, I needed that. I needed to bleed it out. And if it helps even one person feel less alone —or brave enough to ask for help—it was worth every tear.

Writing did something talking never could: it helped me piece it all together. Stuff I hadn't thought about since I was a kid came rushing back—some of it hilarious, some of it completely fucked. I didn't include everything. Mostly because I didn't want to give my mom a heart attack. Some things are just meant to be left alone. Maybe that's the sequel.

The truth is, I've been running from my childhood for most of my life. I tried to outdrink it, outwork it, out joke it—hell, I even tried to outrun it in a pair of size-too-small cowboy boots and a bum knee. None of it worked.

Turns out, the only way to stop dragging your past behind you like a busted kite is to turn around and face it.

So that's what this book is: me turning around.

It's about growing up in a house where love and dysfunction shared a bathroom. It's about chasing normal like the late kid chasing the school bus. About learning to laugh at the worst moments—because if I didn't, they'd eat me alive.

And yeah, it's about addiction. But more than that, it's about the lies we tell ourselves to survive... and the truth that sets us free—after it drags us through the mud first.

If you're reading this because you've ever felt broken, invisible, not enough—or like your life is being written by a sitcom writer on a three-day bender—welcome. You're not alone.

There's no grand lesson here. No twelve-step manual. No list of affirmations with butterfly emojis. Just my story. Told the way I remember it—or the way it made me feel. Sometimes both. Sometimes neither. Memory's weird like that.

But I'll tell you this much:

Sometimes the punchline is the lifeline.

Sometimes the laughter is the scar tissue.

And sometimes, breaking is the beginning.

So let's break some fucking glass.

—Jason Mayo

*"The memories of my childhood are like a nasty car wreck—millions of tiny fragments of shattered glass and twisted metal scattered all over the highway. You can see the pieces, but you can't quite tell what happened, whose fault it was, or if anyone even made it out alive. You just know it was bad. Really bad."*

# Part One
# I'm Fine

# Broken Glass and Bathrobes

I have very little memory of my dad being in the house when I was growing up. Almost none. I'm talking full-on *Gilligan's Island* coconut-to-the-head memory loss stuff. Some scraps of memory and vague feelings linger, but I can't really put them together. I remember living in Rosedale, Queens, when I was about five. We lived in a two-family house close to both sets of grandparents. I had a couple of friends—Ricky and Anthony. I've seen a picture of the three of us sitting on the front stoop. Classic '70s snapshot. I'm not even sure I actually remember being there, or if it's just the photo I remember. It's all fuzzy.

I do remember my dad bringing home a stray German Shepherd we named Pepper. We had him for a few weeks, and then he ran away. That's pretty much the extent of my memories from Rosedale.

When I was about six, we moved to Long Island. My parents bought the house from a family named Ornauer. I remember the smell of the place when we first moved in. It's hard to describe a smell from memory, but it was the kind that sticks with you. Not bad, just... foreign. Like a mix of honey and cough medicine. I can't summon the exact scent anymore—not in an olfactory way—but I'll never forget it.

The brain is wild like that.

This is where things get dicey. I have zero recollection of my little brother existing at that age. I know that sounds harsh, but it is what it is. We're about four-and-a-half years apart, so I guess we didn't have much in common yet—aside from maybe a shared appreciation for applesauce. That would change eventually.

But my dad? I don't remember him being around at all. Like, *ever*. No "Honey, I'm home!" moments. No playing catch. No family road trips. No dinners together. I don't remember celebrating a single holiday with him—not Thanksgiving, not the Fourth of July, not even opening presents with him on Hanukkah. And for a Jewish kid growing up on Long Island, that's kind of a big deal.

I can count on one hand the memories I have of him actually living with us. I vaguely remember him yelling from outside my bedroom window, telling me to come downstairs because he had bought me a record player and a couple of albums—*KISS Destroyer* and *Saturday Night Fever*. That was badass. No wonder I remember it.

I also remember my parents having another couple over for New Year's Eve—getting a little loud and tipsy. And I remember sitting at the dining room table one night, freaking out over a plate of tri-colored pasta. I only wanted to eat one color. My dad made me close my eyes and told me that if I could tell the difference, I could eat whichever one I wanted. That was some stealthy parenting.

But that's pretty much it.

Except for one last memory. And it's a doozy.

I must've been around nine. My brother would've been about four and a half. I know it was nighttime because my parents were both in bathrobes—my dad in a light blue one, my mom in red plaid. We were all sitting in the den. My dad was in his leather recliner, my mom on the couch with us. The vibe was... off. It was quiet. Serious. There wasn't much eye contact, and my mom looked like she was holding back a tidal wave—sad, angry, detached. She didn't want to be there.

If I were older, I would've thought someone was about to tell us they were dying. But my brother and I were clueless. I knew something was wrong, but I didn't know what.

My dad started talking. Calm. Matter-of-fact. My mom didn't say a word. She sat there like a statue. Like she'd lost the ability to speak—or maybe she just didn't have a say in how this went down.

He said: "Your mother and I are getting a divorce. It's not your fault. We both love you very much."

I remember looking at my little brother and feeling bad for him. He didn't get it. He didn't even know what the word *divorce* meant. He was just a baby. I remember thinking, *This isn't fair. This can't really be happening.* I felt unsafe. Afraid. I remember wondering if my dad didn't love us anymore.

After that, everything went blank.

# Spankings and Shit Storms

I t wasn't long before my dad moved out of the house. The worst part was how quickly everything unraveled. There was no transition, no four-point plan, no instruction manual on adapting to a broken home. There was no *Shit Storm for Dummies* available at Barnes & Noble. I was very confused, scared, and embarrassed. So, I can only imagine what my mom was feeling. I was in the third grade at the time. At that age, a kid's only stress should be learning the multiplication tables or navigating the Dewey Decimal System. I went from honing my kickball skills to wondering how my schoolmates, teachers, and other family members would react. Will everyone judge us? Will people gossip about us? Will we be poor? How often will I see my dad? The sudden change and upheaval became a source of anxiety for me, and all the while, I was trying to play it cool like everything was okay.

My mom's demeanor changed almost immediately. At first, she was melancholy. Just kind of sad and removed, but I could tell she was trying her best to hold herself together. I'm sure she was in denial. It's a huge deal when your whole world is turned upside down.

There's only so much one can take. My dad handled all the discipline in the house. That was his role. Those were the days when parents spanked their kids. My dad wasn't a scary or intimidating guy—kind of a working man's Mike Brady. But when he got angry, it was a different story. He was about six feet one inch and 215 pounds, so a spanking wasn't just a light pat on the tush—it had some weight behind it.

He would hold me in place, pull my pants down to expose my butt, and deliver a formidable five-finger slap that left a mark. A good spanking is an art. You have to have the control to make contact just hard enough for your kid to remember but not hard enough to do any serious damage. The spanking itself wasn't even the worst part. It was the whole running for my life thing that preceded it. Trying to get away, hyperventilating, arms flailing like a stuntman falling from a rooftop and the high-pitched screaming. It was like getting chased by a swarm of wasps that wouldn't relent. Jesus, I'm stressing out just thinking about it. Call me a snowflake but I could never do that to my kids.

With my dad gone, my mom's role suddenly changed. She had to go from stay-at-home mom to provider and disciplinarian. When someone's role changes like that, you lose your whole identity. It wasn't fair. She had to go from good cop to bad cop, and that sucks. Kids hate bad cops, and it wasn't any different for us. The whole dynamic got fucked.

My brother and I started to act out. We got mouthy—"fresh," as my mom would say. I refused to listen to her, and my little brother followed my lead like a shadow with a bad attitude. That only made things worse. My mom was at her limit, and her resentment toward my dad started to pour out. She didn't hold back. She'd bad-mouth him constantly, telling us over and over that he was the one who walked out, not her. That this mess was his fault. That our anger should be aimed at him, not her.

And my personal favorite: *If you don't like it, you can go live with him.*

At the time, it didn't feel like a real option—it felt like a threat. Like love had conditions I didn't understand.

I don't know the specifics about child support and alimony, but I was certainly made to feel that whatever it was wasn't nearly enough to support us. My mom was always stressed out about money. She was always worried about not being able to pay the bills. She constantly told us that she didn't know how we would survive.

If you ask my dad, though, he'll tell you he got absolutely railroaded. Like he showed up with a public defender and she rolled in with F. Lee Bailey. The alimony deal? Pay until she got remarried—which, conveniently, never happened. He's convinced she stayed single just to keep him financially neutered, like a cash-dispensing eunuch. She finally let him off the hook when I was in my late thirties, maybe early forties. That alimony lasted longer than their marriage.

# The Family on the Wall

The uneasiness in our home was palpable. I knew my mom was trying her best to hold it all together, but it wasn't hard to see that she was slowly coming undone.

Here I was, a nine-year-old kid, feeling the weight of the world on my shoulders. I worried about my mom, and I felt terrible for my little brother. I wasn't old enough to understand the *why* behind the *what*, but I felt a certain responsibility to keep what was left of our family intact. I had essentially become the little man of the house.

There were pictures hanging on the wall in the hallway by our downstairs bathroom. They were really nice photographs—some in color, some black-and-white. My dad had a thing for taking pictures. He had a fancy camera that looked like something you'd find at the Kennedy Space Center. More than the gear, he had an eye for composition.

Most of the photos were of me and my mom. And she looked so happy in them. There weren't many pictures of my brother. I assume that by the time he was born, my dad had already started to lose interest. And glaringly missing from that wall: a single photo of the four of us together. Not one.

I always wondered if that was on purpose. If my dad already knew he wouldn't be sticking around.

There was no Photoshop back then. No cropping him out. Just a wall of pictures where his absence felt louder than his presence ever had. I found myself wondering about the conversations that happened before, during, and after he'd snapped those photos. The way she looked at me in them—and the way I looked back at her—it might as well have been another lifetime.

It felt so far away.

As time went on, the people in those pictures started to seem like strangers. They became a constant reminder of what our family wasn't.

Happy.

No new pictures ever went up on that wall.

It was as if time had frozen.

# The Poconos and the Forbidden Titties

It didn't take long for my dad to move on. He swapped out our family like a broken appliance—disconnected, discarded, replaced.

Instead of sticking around the neighborhood—renting a condo, crashing in some sad little basement apartment like other newly divorced dads—he decided to pack up and move out of state. *Fucking Connecticut.* As far away from us as possible. *Welcome to Parenting 001: Now You See Me, Now You Don't.*

At the time, I thought of Connecticut as a punishment. Like, "Eat your vegetables or we're sending you to Connecticut." But I learned fast—because that two-hour drive in his shitty little Datsun B-210 became part of the new normal.

We didn't even want to go with him. It was weird from the start. Now we were being shipped off to some faraway land like misfit cargo. Visiting my dad always felt like a trek, and once we got there, it never felt like *ours*. It never felt like "home." No friends. No comfort. It just sucked.

I remember heading to his place for the first time. I was hoping for a *Diff'rent Strokes* moment—Willis and Arnold getting picked up in a limo, whisked away to a penthouse apartment with a spiral staircase, and Mrs. Garrett waiting inside with snacks and a hug.

Nope.

We pulled up to a basic apartment building. I vaguely remember the parking lot, walking up the stairs, and stepping into an underwhelming space. Small kitchen to the left, one main room, and... one bedroom.

*Uh, one bedroom?* So... where were my brother and I supposed to sleep?

Answer: a high-rise trundle bed. One of those beds made to look luxurious but is really just engineered misery. Every time you moved, it squeaked. The springs sank in the middle, so you felt like an accordion. And no matter how you lay, the steel bar was trying to murder you in your sleep.

Way to go, Pops.

Pretty sure he didn't even have a TV at first. To a kid, that's the same as taking away oxygen. There were no snacks. Total bachelor-pad vibes. Like if Greg Brady got married, had kids, got divorced, and then moved back into his groovy crash pad.

The only cool thing was a giant '70s-style beanbag chair. My brother and I would fight over it. He never stood a chance.

We had to do the visit-every-other-weekend, and we dreaded it every single time.

As the months passed and we got a little more familiar with the Connecticut arrangement, my dad dropped another bomb on us. No warning. Just *boom.* He casually informed us he'd been "seeing some-one." A woman. She'd soon be around more. He assured us she wasn't our mother, and he didn't expect us to treat her like one—but she was part of the deal now.

*Bruh. What the actual fuck?*

We met her for the first time on a summer trip to the Poconos. Now, I didn't know much about the Poconos except for the Mount Airy Lodge commercials that ran during reruns of *Three's Company*. Catchy little jingle:

*"Beau-ti-ful Mount Air-y Lodge!"*

Maybe that's where we were going. Maybe Dad was finally doing something right.

Nope.

We ended up at a lake house. Not rat-infested or anything, but it was *definitely* no Mount Airy Lodge.

We were sharing the place with my Uncle Bill, his son Alan (who I actually liked), and Bill's new girlfriend, Sally. Apparently, it was a dad trend to dump your family and shack up with a newer, shinier version of your wife. Cool.

My dad's girlfriend's name? Dominique.

I shit you not.

She was from Paris. *France.* Like, the actual country, not Texas. You can't make this shit up.

My mom didn't even know about her yet. My dad left *that* little reveal to us. "Go ahead and tell your mother." Thoughtful.

Dominique had blond hair, big blue eyes, and a thick French accent I could barely understand. I remember her asking me to change the "shits" on my bed. I think she meant sheets, but all I heard was *shits*.

I laughed. "What? My 'shits' are dirty?"

She didn't think it was funny. I thought it was *hysterical*. I think my dad did, too, but Dominique hit him with the death stare, and he shut it down. Which stung. That moment said a lot—him picking *her side* over mine, even in something harmless.

It wasn't just a dad trying to keep the peace. It was a punch in the gut. A reminder: he'd left. And now I wasn't even sure I was welcome in his new setup. That feeling only grew stronger the longer she stuck around.

The weekend itself wasn't total hell. There was a rec area with basketball courts, a canteen with snacks, and a tabletop *Ms. Pac-Man* game that was elite. The song "Devil Went Down to Georgia" played on repeat. That thing slapped. Still does.

The first full day, Alan, my brother, and I were getting ready to hit the rec center. Anything to avoid the awkward backyard hangout with the new rent-a-moms.

Our bedroom had a big window that looked out onto the lake, and while we were getting dressed, we noticed two women lying in the backyard.

**Topless.**

Yeah. *Topless.*

Boobies. Titties. Badonkers. Bazongas. Chesticles. Over-the-shoulder boulders. Tatty Bojangles.

We freaked out. None of us had ever seen actual boobs before. At least not the kind that didn't belong to our mom (accidentally). These were *real*, live, full-sun boobs. It was like a gift from the divorce gods. We were stunned silent, thankful, confused. This was paradise.

Should we warn our dads?

Nah. That might chase the boobies away.

Then one of them stood up. Turned around.

And that's when I saw her. (And she saw me.)

Dominique.

The "shits" lady.

My dad's girlfriend.

*Jesus Christ.*

Talk about a boner killer.

They weren't just random boobs. They were *forbidden* boobs. Forbidden, awkward, totally traumatizing French boobs. My very first topless sighting—and it was Dominique.

You sank my battleship!

You sank my *battle shit.*

We went from being the luckiest kids on earth to *le petit perverts* in a matter of seconds.

Dominique wasn't thrilled. Neither was I.

And that was only the beginning.

That was the first time I realized my dad hadn't just left—he'd *replaced us.*

And he wanted us to smile about it. To accept it.

So I did what I always did: I laughed. I made jokes about shits and boobs and beanbags and "Devil Went Down to Georgia."

But a seed was planted that day.

If I wasn't the son he wanted—

then I'd learn to be the one who didn't give a shit.

A few years later, Dominique got pregnant.

My dad made *me* tell my mom. I don't remember the exact words he told me to say—I just remember Mom's face when I said them. She started crying. Not the quiet kind, either. The kind that made me want to crawl out of my skin.

The night my sister was born, he left me, my brother, and my friend alone in the house while he took Dominique to the hospital. We stayed up watching *Delirious* on HBO and flipping through MTV like it was some kind of escape hatch.

I didn't know it yet, but that night was a crossroads. A new family had been created. And we weren't part of it.

I love my sister now. I really do. She's one of the best things that came out of all of it.

But back then, it just felt like we'd been left behind—and the next chapter was already being written without us.

# Over the Fence and Under the Stairs

My brother and I fought all the time. He annoyed the shit out of me, and I tortured him. My God-given right as a big brother and his rite of passage as a little brother.

I remember we used to play a game where the sole objective was to throw him over the fence in our backyard. That's it. Just pick him up and launch him over the fence like I was disposing of an old mattress at the local dump. It sounds fucked up, but I think he actually liked it.

There was also the time I made him watch the movie *Carrie*—arguably one of the most frightening movies ever made. He was probably about five or six at the time. I'd issue a spoiler alert, but if you haven't seen a movie that debuted in 1976, you're shit out of luck. There's definitely a statute of limitations on that kind of thing.

We had a basement, and it wasn't finished at the time. Just your run-of-the-mill, creepy-ass basement. Could've easily been the set for *Saw*. The stairs were open in the back, so if you were standing underneath them, you could reach your hand through the slats.

At the end of *Carrie,* there's a dream sequence where the lone survivor is kneeling at Carrie's grave. It's eerily peaceful... until Carrie's dead hand shoots out of the dirt and grabs her. That scene haunted the both of us. So naturally, I set up camp under the stairs and called for my brother to come down.

He did whatever I told him—because, well... big brother.

Just as he hit the middle of the staircase (the point of no return), I shut off the lights, reached through the stairs, and screamed bloody murder as I grabbed his ankle.

If he wasn't traumatized enough from the divorce and the backyard fence tossing, I definitely tied up those loose ends for him.

Apparently, it stuck with him—so much so that during his best man's speech at my wedding, he recounted the story, just to make sure everyone knew what a little shit I was. Good times.

I don't think we fought any more than most brothers do. It was typical stuff. But having a brother made it a little easier to cope with all the chaos. We laughed a lot. I think tickling was a big thing back then. I'm not sure tickling is as popular these days—phones have pretty much taken over.

(If there were a tickling app, I'd probably download it.)

My dad used to tickle us. That man was a master tickler. He had a sixth sense for it—like acupuncture for your funny bone. He found this spot on the sides of our knees that would make us lose our shit. He could tickle both of us at once. Ambidextrous tickling could've been an Olympic sport. I'd watch the hell out of that.

When my dad was gone, I tried to take over some of that responsibility. There was no Mr. Miyagi training montage for becoming the man of the house. No big brother to father figure boot camp. But I tried.

As a kid, you don't think about things like trauma or PTSD. As an adult, you usually associate trauma with soldiers coming home from war or survivors of domestic violence. But I know now—*really* know —that trauma comes in many forms.

Being a child of divorce is a legit form of trauma. It took years of therapy to say that out loud without shame.

Having a brother gave us a shared experience. A secret language. A co-conspirator. We were trauma bonding long before we knew what that meant.

And you know what? We still do. It's not a bad thing.

We were lucky to have each other. And we still are.

# You Say Night, I Say Mare

These weren't the typical kid nightmares with monsters hiding under the bed or poison apple-type shit. These were full-blown, melt-your-fucking-skull anxiety dreams. You'd think I was selling stocks on Black Thursday for a living back in 1929. Nope. Just a kid whose parents split up.

My earliest memory of these nightmares was when my dad was still living with us. He wasn't around much, but I think he was technically still there. I have a lot of memories like that—vague, foggy, uncertain.

For a long time, I assumed the lack of clarity was because the memories were too painful to process, that my brain was repressing them as a defense mechanism.

Turns out that wasn't the case.

Years later, when I brought it up with my dad, he confirmed it: He just wasn't around. No fancy psychological explanation. No mind doing somersaults to protect me. The dude was just absent. Period. He just didn't want to be at the house. He either said he was working late or stayed at friends' houses to avoid coming home.

I figured out at one point that I could've saved approximately $140,000 in therapy if he had just told me that sooner. Fucker.

On some level, that actually made me feel a little better. For a long time, I was writing my own narrative to help put the pieces of the puzzle together. This made it way more simple.

With that being said, my brain still needed an outlet—especially because I wasn't talking about it with anyone. During the day, I tried to just push my feelings away. Sweep them under the rug, or—since it was the 1970s—the shag carpet.

So my anxiety came out at night. When I was asleep. It came in the form of nightmares.

*Really fucking scary* nightmares.

My brother and I were sharing a room upstairs. That's when they started. Same one, over and over and over again.

This is how it went...

*There's a huge field. It's lush and filled with really tall dandelions. The sky is clear and blue and as bright as any perfect spring day. A little girl is standing in the middle of the field. She's wearing an adorable yellow polka-dot sundress. She's barely tall enough to see over the dandelions, but I can see her.*

*It's peaceful. Tranquil. Sublime, even. The exact opposite of what my life feels like during the day.*

*What happens next is the mare part of the nightmare.*

*Things slowly become more ominous in the field. Nothing about the picture itself changes. It's just the... aura. It's really hard to describe because there's no audible change, either. Just the exact setting.*

*But a feeling of dread starts to percolate.*

*It's not happening to her. It's happening around her. In spite of her.*

*It's like the Jaws theme and a ticking time bomb are having a baby.*

*The slow creep. The rising dread. The countdown I can't stop.*

*Now take all of that away. No music. No ticking. Just quiet.*

*And somehow... it's worse.*

*Because it's not outside me anymore.*

*It's inside.*

*And it's not going anywhere.*

*The juxtaposition of the perfect little girl in her perfect yellow sundress, surrounded by those beautiful dandelions—and the feeling of absolute helplessness and doom just rolling in like a fog. It's as if I know something terrible, something horrifying, is about to happen. But it just keeps going. So the dread keeps creeping up on her. Creeping up on me.*

*Until I feel the fear strangling me like barbed wire wrapped around my throat.*

That was the dream. Always the same.

So I was powerless during the day and even when I was asleep.

But it wasn't just me.

After my dad left, my mom started having nightmares, too. Only hers were louder.

When my mom had bad dreams, she'd scream in her sleep—but not like a horror movie scream. It was more like a high-pitched moan that slowly built until it filled the whole house—almost operatic. And because she was hard of hearing and slept without her hearing aids, she couldn't hear me or my brother yelling for her to wake up.

So I'd have to do it. Get out of bed, in the dark, heart racing, and walk down the hallway alone to shake her out of it. It was awful. I dreaded it. The sound, the silence after, the guilt of waking her up, the weight of being the one who had to do it.

That went on for years. It was worse right after the divorce, when everything still felt upside-down. Her dreams weren't just her dreams —they became mine too. And no matter how many times I made that walk to her bedroom, it never got easier.

But her screams weren't the only ones. Mine came too.

Some nights I would wake up on my own. Other nights, I would scream so loud that my mom probably thought Beelzebub himself had jumped through the window and landed on my bed.

Sometimes, I would wake up and hide behind my closet door with my eyes squeezed shut, unable to speak or breathe.

Daytime was exhausting.

But nighttime? That was a swift kick to my little man-balls.

**P.S.**

It took me years to figure out where that nightmare might've come from.

Turns out, I probably saw something on TV when I was a kid.

A political ad called "Daisy Girl."

A little girl in a field, picking petals.

Then a countdown.

Then a nuclear bomb.

My anxious little subconscious must've grabbed that imagery and mixed it with everything I was already feeling—powerlessness, dread, the fear that things could change in an instant and there'd be nothing I could do.

Google it—if you're in the mood to ruin your day.

Or your childhood.

Or both.

# The Turtleneck Chronicles

W
e lived in a pretty well-off town. Most of the kids at school lived in nice houses and dressed in nice clothes. They had Atari, cable TV, and Betamax machines—but we didn't.

I remember taking notice of some of the apparel the other kids were sporting. Everyone was wearing Benetton, Lacoste, and velour sweat suits. They had all the accouterments—Swatch watches and Jelly Shoes. They were traipsing through the mall, hitting up Members Only, while I was wandering the aisles of the local Army and Navy store, feeling out of place in my turtleneck and corduroys.

There was one time my mom took me shopping and I got to pick out a couple of outfits. There were these pants that were maroon with a gray stripe down the side and a maroon and gray shirt to match. I got the same outfit in black and red. I was so happy wearing those clothes. For a time, it made me feel normal.

I was a big Rangers fan, and everyone else on Long Island was an Islanders fan, so I would often get chastised at school by everyone.

The Rangers were a shit team back then, and the Islanders were just beginning what turned out to be a dynasty. Terrible timing.

If that wasn't bad enough, I had to listen to games on the radio while the other guys watched on SportsChannel. That might not sound like a big deal, but to a kid—it's everything. I used to pretend I watched the game, hoping nobody would find out. All I wanted was to blend in, and it wasn't easy.

Being around other kids—and even their parents—was always uncomfortable. I couldn't help but think they were judging me. I felt like an outsider, like I didn't belong there.

My mom got a job, but it wasn't a career, and she struggled to make ends meet. Later, I learned she was an incredible artist. She actually went to Pratt to become an interior designer, but she abandoned that path for my father so she could stay at home with us. I'm sure that only fed her resentment for him—and who could blame her?

As my behavior got worse, I think my mom started to worry about my mental state. I wasn't communicating with her, and I was always angry. My teachers must have noticed, too, and become concerned because I started getting pulled into the guidance counselor's office every week.

I don't remember much at all about that. I remember what she looked like and that her name was Mrs. Solomon. She was very nice, but I'm sure I didn't speak much during our visits—if at all.

This was probably the beginning of my tendency to detach and withdraw from anyone who tried to help me. I just couldn't communicate honestly, and I was vulnerable at the time. I was nine, for Christ's sake. I always felt awkward and uneasy. I didn't know why. I just did.

What made it worse was that I actually *wanted* to talk. Like, really badly. Every time someone asked if I was okay, all I could think was,

*No, I'm not okay. Please fucking make it okay.* But I couldn't say it. I don't know if it was shame or the fear that saying it out loud would make it too real—but the words just wouldn't come. And then I'd feel even worse. Not just for myself, but because I could tell the person trying to help felt helpless. Like I was letting them down for not opening up. That pattern—pushing away the people who loved me most—started then. And it stuck with me straight through adulthood.

Around the same time as my stint with the guidance counselor, my mom also sent me to therapy. The details are fuzzy, but I remember my therapist. She was an older woman, probably in her fifties—but at the time, I probably thought she was ancient. She was short, and her posture was terrible. Always hunched over. That alone was weird to me.

I remember her trying to make conversation, but I never wanted to talk about anything. She'd try to engage me with everyday stuff. I had pet newts at the time that I loved. One time, I brought them in a big Tupperware and just played with them during our session.

I also remember her taking me for walks outside. Probably to get me in a more comfortable environment. Thinking about it now, I find it both hilarious and kind of adorable. She was probably a great therapist—but again, I just wasn't ready to open up to anyone.

That relationship didn't last very long.

I didn't want help. I just wanted things to stop falling apart.

# The Night I Almost Murdered
# Mrs. Curtain

As all of this was going on, there was another bit of cash and prizes added to the pot of shit that was my life.

Because money was so tight, my mom was getting more and more anxious, and she was having trouble keeping up. In addition to her job, we had a little help from my grandparents, which always felt like a safety net to me—but it still wasn't enough.

I'm not sure where she got the idea from—maybe one of her single mom friends. They ran in packs back then. My mom was part of a group called Parents Without Partners. Just reading that back makes me snort and cry at the same time.

"Hey, where's your mom?"

"Oh, she's at her Parents Without Partners meeting."

"Huh?"

"Oh never mind. Let's just play hide and seek." Emphasis on the *hide*.

Anyway, my mom decided she would rent out the upstairs of our house for some extra cash. It wasn't exactly legal unless you had permits or whatever, but it wasn't uncommon either. There are probably a bunch of single old women real estate moguls out there sitting on a pile of cash.

In order to do this, things would have to change. Again.

This time, instead of my world turning upside down, it took a ride on the Tilt-a-Whirl. Insert mental and emotional vomit here.

In what seemed like overnight, my cousin Joe—and maybe even my Zeide—came over and did a makeshift version of *This Old House*. They built a sheetrock wall at the front of our living room that created a separate-but-shared entryway, so someone could get upstairs without us having to scramble in our tighty-whities every time they came "home." They also added a little kitchenette upstairs and turned it into a sweet little bachelor pad.

That also meant I was evicted from my own room without warning. If that happened today, I'd have squatters' rights. I probably could've taken my mom to court and sued her for an old couch or something. But I was a team player.

The living part wasn't as bad as I thought it would be. My brother and I already shared a room. We were moved downstairs to a smaller room that used to be something else—but I don't remember what. To compensate, my mom bought us a dope bunk bed. That part was cool.

But that was the *only* cool part.

Now, already feeling ashamed and different, I was the kid living in a house-turned-other-house, with a stranger moving in because his family was poor. That would definitely get me the chicks.

More shame. More embarrassment. A heaping tablespoon of humiliation.

A three-ingredient shit cake.

Eat up.

The first tenant—and there were several over the years—was a lady named Mrs. Curtain. There couldn't have been a worse fit. She was old, mean-looking, and smelled like mothballs.

I mean, why couldn't it have been a cool, middle-aged divorced dude who fell in love with my mom and we lived happily ever after? That would've been some awesome Venus flytrap-type shit.

Or even a twentysomething, blond, Swedish exchange student who had a thing for awkward, freckle-faced, broken kids.

Wishful thinking. But a kid can dream, right?

When Mrs. Curtain moved in, it was exactly like I thought it would be. I felt like an unwanted guest in my own home, and I never had anyone over because I was embarrassed. My close friends from the block were allowed, because they were part of the honorary Children Without Parents Living Together group—but for everyone else, it was off-limits.

Kind of like a less-than-top-secret Area 51... in a nice Jewish neighborhood.

I was still having nightmares at the time. Later in life, I found out they were actually night terrors. I also found out that night terrors can manifest in many forms. Like sleepwalking.

I'm sure you can guess where this is headed.

Well... you're probably right. But it's actually worse—and hilarious at the same time. Not for Mrs. Curtain, but for me, all these years later? Top-tier comedy.

One night, when everyone was asleep, I guess I was having one of these high-octane night terrors and decided to sleepwalk *upstairs* to Mrs. Curtain's apartment.

But not before making a pit stop at my mom's desk, opening the drawer, and grabbing a letter opener. For all you young people out there who don't know what a letter opener is: it's a sharp, long tool used to open envelopes without tearing them. Basically... a high-end prison shiv.

So there I am, creeping up the stairs like Jason Voorhees from *Friday the 13th*, letter opener in hand, straight to Mrs. Curtain's bed. I then stood over her—still as a scarecrow—letter opener raised, in striking position.

Thank God she woke up before I went full *Children of the Corn* on her.

I'm sure *terrified* doesn't even begin to describe what she felt. Suffice it to say, Mrs. Curtain didn't stick around too long after that.

I mean... in my defense—lock your fucking door, lady.

What I really needed that night wasn't a letter opener.

I needed a role model. A guide. Someone to show me what the hell to do with all the confusion and anger swirling around inside me.

But there wasn't one. So I did what I always did.

I made it up as I went along.

# Jack Tripper and The Latchkey Kids

Most kids grow up with heroes they look up to. Someone to model yourself after. Back in the '70s and '80s, most of the kids I hung out with were either obsessed with *Star Wars*, the Yankees, or the Pittsburgh Steelers—shout out to the Steel Curtain (no relation to Mrs. Curtain). So you were either Team Han or Team Luke, Bucky Dent or Rich "The Goose" Gossage, or all-in on Mean Joe Greene.

Me personally? I was a San Diego Chargers fan. Don't ask. So I loved Kellen Winslow, Dan Fouts, and Charlie Joiner. I actually still have my Wes Chandler jersey. It's in perfect condition. Fits me like a crop top now, but I'll cherish it forever.

I loved watching those guys and definitely tried—unsuccessfully—to emulate their play at the schoolyard, but I didn't really look up to them. They weren't role models. I only saw my dad every other weekend, so there was no mini-me type thing. He didn't give me a pat on the ass before the game and say, *Go get 'em, son.* And he definitely didn't give me the ol' birds-and-the-bees talk. Once, my mom asked me if I used condoms, and that was about it. I was seventeen.

My role model was a bit more unconventional.

Because my mom worked full-time, we had to get ourselves to and from school on our own. It was only a few blocks away. In those days, it wasn't uncommon for kids to fend for themselves. We were Gen X, for God's sake. We almost died every time we left the house, and nobody batted an eyelash. We were the Latchkey Kids. Sounds like a cheesy sitcom, but it was our reality.

For those who don't know, a Latchkey Kid is basically a kid whose parents both work, so they've got their own key to let themselves in and out of the house. You don't see much of that these days. Jeez, I don't think *my* daughters' feet touched pavement until they were eighteen.

Aside from letting ourselves in and out, we also had to keep ourselves busy before our mom got home. This is where my brother and I really started to bond. We watched a ton of TV and ate a shitload of Honeycombs. TV was the best back then—pure cheeseball. Post–*Leave It to Beaver* stuff. *Gilligan's Island* (Ginger was definitely a formative part of my childhood), *The Brady Bunch, Batman*—the '60s version with Adam West confidently rocking a dad bod in that clingy Batsuit—and probably the most important: *Three's Company.*

It was funny, had one-and-a-half super-hot chicks (sorry, Joyce DeWitt), was incredibly racy for its time, and featured without a doubt the most influential male figure of my childhood:

Jack. Fucking. Tripper.

That's right. He was an absolute legend. Good-looking but not too slick, hysterically funny, smooth with the ladies, and, most of all, an all-around solid guy. He was sensitive and kind. He always did the right thing by his friends—even Mr. Roper, who was probably the most homophobic, curmudgeon, old fart this side of Archie Bunker.

Okay, so Jack's entire existence was based on a lie to convince his landlord he wasn't pimping out Janet and Chrissy. But his motives were always good.

My brother and I watched every single episode on repeat. Jack was a beacon of light in an otherwise dimly lit time for us. For thirty minutes, we scarfed oversized Tupperware containers of cold cereal and laughed our butts off, even though half the jokes were sexual innuendos that we didn't understand.

He taught me how to problem-solve—even if the problems were completely avoidable and insanely stupid. He taught me not to take myself too seriously (which, in hindsight, turned into more of a self-defense mechanism in the form of self-deprecation). He taught me how to be kind, and that you always try to do the right thing—or come clean, no matter what.

But more than that, the show gave me *permission*. Permission to laugh. To mess up. To fall down the stairs or say something dumb or slam the door because of a misunderstanding—and not get punished for it. Just cue the laugh track, cut to commercial, and try again.

It might sound far-fetched, but my brother and I still worship him. We both have THE REGAL BEAGLE T-shirts. And aside from Chris Cornell, he's the only celebrity I ever bawled my eyes out over when he died.

Honestly, *Three's Company* probably also subconsciously introduced me to drinking—given how much time they spent at The Beagle.

And Chrissy? Total smoke show. Marone.

# Prince Fucking Chulalongkorn

There's one moment in time that really stands out as a mini respite from the delicate facade I was struggling to manage.

Actually—fuck that.

It wasn't just a mini respite. It was more like an all-expenses-paid vacation on the most audacious, all-inclusive Disney Dream Cruise you could possibly imagine.

I was in the fifth grade and already had a couple of years of divorce boot camp under my belt. I was trudging through elementary school like a three-legged turtle. The weight of it all was exhausting. My attention span and aptitude for things like multiplication and long division were fading fast. It was getting harder and harder to concentrate. The more I buried my feelings, the heavier they got.

My teacher was Mrs. Carter. She was different from my other teachers. She was super pretty—like a straight-edge version of Farrah Fawcett with brown hair and brown eyes. She was intimidating, but not in a scary way. It was the way she carried herself. She seemed confident, poised, and graceful. When she spoke, we listened. There was something really different about her. She made me feel comfortable.

A few weeks into the school year, she announced that our class would be doing the school play: a full-on production of *The King and I*. I had no clue what the hell that was, but I did know it meant I would have to get up in front of the entire school and prance around like an idiot in some stupid costume.

It sounded like my worst nightmare. Just what I needed—another opportunity to feel vulnerable and embarrassed. I wanted to crawl into a dark hole and hide.

One day, she rolled a tall, two-tier cart into the classroom with a TV and a VCR all set up. We watched the movie version of *The King and I* starring Yul Brynner. It wasn't nearly as terrible as I anticipated. Suddenly, my mood went from cynical to curious.

She told us there would be tryouts the following week. Anyone who didn't get a main part would be in the ensemble or work backstage. The idea of being a stagehand sounded about right. I could participate with minimal risk of having a nervous breakdown. Hovering in the background was the path of least resistance. I'll do that.

But that's not at all what Mrs. Carter had in mind. She had a much different plan.

David Weinberger was the most popular boy in the fifth grade. He was in a serious relationship with Sidney Braunstein, the most popular girl in the fifth grade. They were a hot item. David was outgoing, handsome, and a natural fit for the role of the King.

Mrs. Carter took me aside and asked if I would try out for the role of Prince Chulalongkorn. It was a substantial part—the King's son, for crying out loud. You can't get more substantial than that. If I got the part, there'd be a lot of lines to remember and even a song to sing.

The whole idea seemed really stressful, but it didn't feel like I had much of a choice.

I auditioned for the part—and I fucking nailed it. Song and all.

It was me and David Weinberger on the big stage, under the bright lights.

Maybe this wouldn't be so bad after all.

Turns out, Mrs. Carter knew exactly what she was doing.

Working on that play pretty much took up the entire school year. We were in the auditorium rehearsing what felt like all day, every day. I don't think we learned a damn thing that year. It was the perfect distraction for a kid who wanted to be anywhere but in his own skin.

I wasn't Jason, the eleven-year-old child of divorce.

I was Prince **Fucking** Chulalongkorn, dammit.

Looking back on it now, that might've been the greatest year of my life. I felt wanted, appreciated, accepted, and—most of all—normal. It also started a creative fire in my belly that still burns to this day.

I'll never forget that year or Mrs. Carter. In many ways, she saved me. She'll always hold a special place in my heart.

That was the moment I felt seen—center stage, basking in the glow of acceptance.

I didn't know it yet, but years later I'd chase that feeling again.

Only this time, the stage would be bigger. The stakes would be higher.

And the crash?

Let's just say, it wouldn't end with a standing ovation.

# Boobs, Bad Haircuts, and the Great Escape

Iff fifth grade was the year I got to feel seen, summer was the season I tried to be felt.

My mom managed to send my brother and me to day camp. It wasn't fancy—aka cheap. It was one of those Jewish Federation camps, which sounds frightening. Any sentence with the words *Jewish* and *camp* in it sounds alarming, but here we are.

I never went to a fancy camp, so I didn't know the difference and I didn't really care. I never understood the whole indoor tennis courts and horseback riding bullshit. This was day camp, not *The Flamingo Kid*. But day camp was still cool. There were a lot of sports—and sports were everything back then. Didn't matter which one you played; it was the distraction that counted.

I was never amazing at sports, but I hustled harder than anyone else to compensate. That's what coaches tell a kid's parents when they aren't good: "Johnny's a real hustler. He's got heart. Leaves it all on the field." I heard a lot of that growing up. Sports gave me an outlet. A place to park the chaos from home. I also felt like I had something to prove—and sports gave me a place to showcase the heavy, growing chip I proudly carried on my tiny shoulders.

Camp wasn't just baseball, soccer, and football. There were weird sports you only found at camp—like ga-ga, tetherball, and croquet. These were *camp-only* sports, and under no circumstances were they ever spoken about to non-camp friends. Too hard to explain to an outsider.

You couldn't just say: "Hey, bud, guess what I did today? First we played a sweaty game of ga-ga, then chugged some Bug Juice, then we battled through a grueling Tetherball tourney before finishing off the afternoon with croquet." If I said that out loud anywhere past camp lines, my friends would call me a faggot and throw a stickball bat at my head.

At the start of camp, I wasn't expecting much. I was just glad to be out of the house, hanging with my summer friends and dirtying up my tube socks every day. What I didn't know was that I was about to have the greatest, most epic summer of my life. Not just *up to that point*—I mean of my *entire life*.

Up until then, I wasn't exactly what you'd call a ladies' man. I was twelve. Pale, freckled, below-average muscle tone, with a smile that looked like someone glued oversized yellow Chiclets to my gums. I also had a shit haircut. Actually, I didn't have a haircut. If you look at pictures of me at that age, it's just one giant-ass cowlick. Hideous.

I don't think my mom could afford regular haircuts, and this was pre-Flowbee, so we just went with it. I do remember my mom dating one of the Italian barbers for a while. My hair looked semi-serviceable for the duration of that relationship.

I'd kissed one or two girls in sixth grade. No one was throwing themselves at the poor kid with the shitty haircut, but I did manage a quick mercy kiss or two during a couple awkward games of spin the bottle. And even if they had, I wouldn't have known what to do with them. There was no internet, no boob tube videos. It was straight-up *National Geographic* or squinting at a blurry shred of nipple in Mom's latest issue of *Vogue*.

The summer before eighth grade, my mom signed us up for day camp again. None of my friends from the Children Without Parents Living Together group did day camp or sleepaway camp. I don't know why, but most Jewish kids from Long Island went to camp. Most non-Jewish kids didn't. It wasn't a money thing—we were swimming way below middle class. My theory? Jewish parents wanted to get rid of their asshole kids for the summer. Non-Jewish parents *also* wanted to get rid of their asshole kids—but for some reason, they didn't. They just gave them money for the ice cream truck and sent them to the town pool. Who the fuck knows?

When camp started, everything was copacetic. Sports, soggy chicken fingers, rinse and repeat. But this year, there was something else thrown into the pot:

*Girls.*

Not just any girls—*new* girls. Girls who didn't know me. Girls with no idea I was a freckled, cowlicked, Chiclet-toothed loner.

Sure, I still wasn't a looker—but by this point I had a secret weapon. I had developed a sharp wit, cunning sarcasm, and a full commitment to making people laugh. I think I started coming out of my shell after *The King and I* experience. It was survival. Humor became my armor.

If you were good at being funny, you could control the narrative. You could steer the conversation. You didn't have to be the best at anything—you just had to make everyone forget to notice. It became a full-on persona. I wasn't Jason the Sad Kid anymore. I was the class clown. The loveable smartass.

And it turns out, the girls in camp loved the funny guy.

At that age, everyone looked the same. Buck teeth. Tight shorts. Tube socks. I could write an entire chapter on the tight shorts and tube socks debacle. Jesus, I look at those summer pics, and it looks like my tiny man parts were being butterflied like a shrimp. Prepubescent privates squashed into rayon. It made them look like a raisin sitting on top of a radish.

The tube socks were another level of fashion trauma. An abomination. Half sock, half long john. They looked like motel towels with prison stripes. And we pulled them up *just* below the knee. The higher the sock, the more street cred. They were like sweatpants for your calves. Just awful.

A couple weeks into camp, the girls started hanging with us. Must've been the pheromones. Sweat and salami sandwich breath was our mating call back then.

Somehow I wound up with the "cool" crowd (and I use that term with humble caution). One girl caught my eye. Her name was Jill. Gorgeous. Brown feathered hair. Dark brown eyes. And what, at the time, seemed like a killer body. Oddly enough, the girls and boys wore the same outfits—shorts and T-shirts—but to us, this was like discovering a new galaxy.

Somehow, she and I hit it off. She laughed at my jokes. She was sweet and cute and genuine. I remember her eyes more than anything. There was something mysterious about her. She was the forbidden fruit. My first crush.

We started spending more time together and eventually became an item at camp. We were *infatuated*. I kept waiting for the other shoe to drop. She was my first everything.

Without getting into too much detail (because gentlemen never tell), things got hot and steamy that summer. We made out constantly when no one was looking. We probably looked like two fish fighting for the same worm. Neither of us knew what the hell we were doing.

Sometimes we'd go on day trips, all packed into hot, sweaty school buses. Your thighs would stick to the seats. Zero sex appeal. Still didn't matter.

One day, we went roller skating. Dark rink, loud music, about a hundred kids and maybe five counselors. No eyes on us. We snuck to a corner and made out. And for the first time ever—I touched a boob.

I'm pretty sure it happened by accident... but in an incredible act of kindness, she let me touch it again.

It didn't feel real. But it was.

And for the first time in forever, I felt no worry. No anxiety. No shame. I was on top of the world. She became my escape that summer. I didn't just fall in love with *her*. I fell in love with what she represented—what I *thought* a relationship could give me: salvation.

That idea—that a girl could save me—became a blueprint. A romantic hostage plan I'd repeat over and over again throughout my addiction and depression. I used relationships like duct tape on a leaky pipe, hoping love could fix what nothing ever could.

I think I peaked that summer, at the ripe old age of twelve. I never captured that feeling of lightness again—not for a long time. But for one summer, there was a silver lining.

You know what they say...

Every once in a while, even the darkest clouds will piss rain that makes something grow.

But once I got rolling in middle school—everything got messier—I found something stronger than a summer crush. Something that made me feel bolder, funnier, cooler. Like I finally had a place in the world.

Alcohol.

# Thermoses, Puke, and the Invisibility Cloak

I guess I started drinking heavily when I was about fourteen—probably eighth or ninth grade. We couldn't get beer, so we used to steal alcohol from our parents' closets, liquor cabinets, wherever. I specifically remember stealing liquor from my best friend's front closet. The assortment was never great—usually some kind of whiskey. We all hated it, but it got us buzzed, so we made do.

As we got bolder, we took bigger risks. My friend Duke suggested breaking into his dad's shed, where he supposedly kept all his liquor. So that's what we did. We'd hang out on Friday or Saturday nights, pour everything into a thermos—whiskey, vodka, gin, even some mystery creamy liquor that only old people drank—and hit the streets. It was disgusting, but effective.

We'd stumble around the neighborhood until one of us puked in a bush or passed out on a stranger's lawn. It was like we believed the booze made us invisible—our own version of Harry Potter's cloak of invisibility for drunken teenagers.

One time after a night of thermos cocktails, I woke up in the bathtub with the shower blasting full force. Fully clothed, shoes and all, soaked like a sandwich someone dropped in a puddle.

I didn't just decide to sober up with a cold shower—I had clearly blacked out, time-traveled into the tub, and hit the water like it was some kind of detox chamber.

The next thing I remember is my mom pounding on the bathroom door like the FBI. She must have gotten up to pee and realized I wasn't exactly known for 3 a.m. steam baths.

Half-conscious and still half-drunk, I did what any aspiring teenage alcoholic would do: I lied like it was a survival skill.

I slurred something about a huge fire a few blocks away, claimed the smoke made me sick, and that the steam would help clear it out.

Also handy? It washed the puke off my jeans.

Miraculously, she seemed to buy it—or she just didn't have the energy to deal—and left me alone to marinate in my own stupidity.

I eventually dragged myself out of the tub, soggy and staggering, and crashed into the top bunk like it was just another Friday night.

It sounds insane that thirteen- and fourteen-year-olds were out in full blackout mode with little parental concern, but we were all in "special" situations. Most of us came from broken homes. We lived with our moms, and they had little control over us. We were disrespectful —indifferent at best. I remember my mom chasing me and my little brother around the house with a belt. I'd trap us in a corner and use him as a human shield. Terrifyingly hilarious at the time but never any real consequences.

That went on through middle school. By high school, we got more organized. No fake IDs, but we somehow managed to score beer from 7-Elevens and liquor stores. My go-to was vodka or blackberry brandy in a half-pint. Vodka got OJ. Brandy was straight from the bottle.

What kind of high school kid drinks blackberry brandy anyway? Sounds like something you'd sip at a saloon in the Wild West or in a '70s stakeout van.

Our routine was simple: meet up, drink at the A&P parking lot, then walk drunk to a party across town. We traveled in packs. It felt safe. Normal. Everyone drank. It was a rite of passage.

Sure, there was pressure—get called a pussy or a faggot if you didn't drink—but that didn't faze me. I might've felt pressure to lose my virginity, but drinking? Easy. I *loved* drinking. It made me feel confident, funny. I could talk to anyone, say anything, and fit right in. Being drunk was so much easier than being sober.

Even at fourteen, my drinking was anything but normal. I was a blackout drinker right out of the gate.

But not every memory from back then was soaked in blackberry brandy and stupidity.

Some of it was just... being a kid. Being dumb. Having friends.

There was still some light before the wheels came off.

# Shoot the Puck, Barry

M y best friend at the time was a girl named Stephanie. She was awesome. Our friendship started in elementary school —she had a crush on me. I didn't really think of her that way at the time. Not because she wasn't cute, but because kickball and flipping baseball cards were more important than romance.

She had an older brother named Jack, which was cool because I didn't know any older siblings—just had to deal with being one. I loved going to her house. Her family had Intellivision, which was like the thinking man's Atari. It had better graphics but overly complicated controllers. Playing was like landing a plane, and I was terrible at it. Her brother would let me win, and I appreciated that.

Her dad was a working-class guy. Blunt, not especially warm, but decent. Her mom was one of the kindest people I've ever met. She really looked out for me. Their house felt safe.

Best part? They were die-hard Rangers fans—in a sea of Islanders fans. They had season tickets: four seats, usually only using three. One day, her dad invited me to a game. I was maybe ten. No jersey, no hat, but I bled blue. We took the LIRR to Madison Square Garden. Total chaos. Bar cars, poker games, rowdy drunks. It felt like St. Patrick's Day every day.

Penn Station smelled like beer and piss. Everyone was chanting, "LET'S GO RANGERS!" I was half frightened, half elated. I felt like I belonged. I was a Rangers fan, surrounded by my people. That feeling—of being part of something, of not feeling ashamed—that was a drug all its own. I'd chase it for decades.

The Garden was electric. Their seats were in section 414—the blue seats. Cheap seats. Real fans. We were right above supermodel Carol Alt. When they sang the anthem, we'd chant, "CA-ROL! CA-ROL!" and she'd smile. It was magic.

The crowd was brutal—vulgar, unfiltered. Everyone cursed like drunken sailors. Don Koharski, an overweight ref, got the worst of it: "Eat another fucking donut, Koharski!" Islanders defenseman Dennis Potvin was public enemy #1. Fans chanted, "Beat your wife, Potvin!" and of course, the infamous "Potvin Sucks!" chant—still echoing through the Garden to this day.

Everything happened in the blue seats: gambling, smoking, even coke. Nobody hid it. They'd go to the stairwell, "the well," and light up. Weed, cigarettes, whatever. I didn't know what cocaine was at the time, but I'd soon learn.

My favorite player was Barry Beck. Big, red-headed defenseman with a cannon slapshot. When he touched the puck, the section screamed, "SHOOT THE PUCK, BARRY!" Everyone knew he was my favorite, so they'd yell it at me, too. I loved that. I was part of the tribe.

After Stephanie's dad died of a sudden heart attack, it all changed. It was the first time someone I knew personally died. I was gutted. The games weren't the same without him. I started going less. But I'll always love Stephanie and her family. They gave me a place to feel seen.

Years later, I'd get my own season tickets. The Garden became a huge part of my drinking and drugging. I wanted to be like the guys in the blue seats—and eventually, I was. Just for the wrong reasons.

My first real blackout happened when I was fourteen. I don't remember any of it—just what I was told.

Stephanie and I still talked, even though we didn't hang out as much. One night, after a typical round of binge drinking, I apparently wandered across town to her house—uninvited—at 2 a.m. Nobody locked their doors back then, so I let myself in, walked upstairs, and straight into her mom's bedroom.

She woke up, terrified. Stephanie was mortified. I somehow made it home, no clue what I'd done until Stephanie told me.

I was horrified. Embarrassed. Ashamed. Scared. But the next time I went to Stephanie's house, her mom didn't say a word about it. She spared me the humiliation. That grace stuck with me.

But that was not normal behavior for a fourteen-year-old—let alone anyone. It was an early red flag, one that should've set off alarms for everyone around me. But it didn't. Not really.

Stephanie's mom didn't bring it up. She didn't scold me or call my mom or make a scene. She just... let me off the hook. And I was grateful. Deeply. But looking back now, I see it for what it was: another moment when I got away with it. Another consequence that never fully landed.

It became a pattern—people letting me off the hook, giving me grace I hadn't earned, chalking it up to youth or chaos or "just being a kid." And every time that happened, I sank a little deeper. The shame didn't go away—it just went underground, building up pressure for years.

Eventually, the consequences stopped being optional. They stopped being kind. They showed up with blood and broken glass and ultimatums.

But back then? I was still getting passes. Still slipping by. And every time someone looked the other way, I learned the wrong lesson:

That I could keep doing this.

That I'd always get away with it.

That nothing bad was ever really going to happen.

Until it did.

# Wine Coolers, Lava Lamps, and Shitty Poetry

When I was about fifteen or sixteen, my mother started buying me alcohol. I would persuade her to stock beer and wine coolers in the fridge. The instructions were explicit: Bud Light in cans and Bartles & Jaymes in bottles. I told her all of my friends would be coming over and that we'd hang out in the basement. I guess she figured being home instead of out on the streets would keep us out of trouble. I think her intentions were good, but she was also probably nervous about what I might do if she said no.

There were, in fact, times when my friends and I would hang out and drink that alcohol in my house—but most of the time, I drank it on my own. Usually with no intention of leaving or meeting up with anyone.

The memory of that room still comes to me viscerally. Just like a lot of things, I associate places and objects with feelings and emotions from different time periods in my life. These memories are kind of like photographs tucked away in a dusty album, hidden on a shelf in a room that's been boarded shut.

When my mom told me we could clean out the basement so I could move down there, I was pumped. My brother and I still shared a room with those bunk beds, and I was getting pissed—I needed more space for a shitload of reasons. I mean, I was sixteen. There are only so many showers you can take in a day before your mom starts asking questions. Although I think I might've fallen in love with a bottle of Agree shampoo that year. Don't judge.

Moving down there was awesome. I had my own bed—one of those high-rise contraptions that doubled as a couch during the day. It was small, but I made the most of it. I still had the stereo my dad bought me years ago: a receiver and a turntable for my records. Eventually, cassettes became a thing, so I got a boombox. It was sick—black, with a dual cassette deck so you could record from tape to tape. The speakers were detachable, so you could set it up like a stereo system. Best part? It had equalizers. I even remember the settings: the treble all the way up on the right, the bass about three-quarters on the left, and the mids flat across the board. There was a red digital readout of the track numbers that lit up the room at night. I was so damn proud of that thing. It was probably the first time in my life I was on the cutting edge of anything.

Like any teenage boy, my room was covered in posters. I was a metal guy who secretly loved new wave—thanks to my camp friends. (Another thing that stayed behind camp lines.) My favorite was a huge Manowar poster. The band looked absolutely ridiculous— shirtless, in animal furs and Viking gear. Extremely homoerotic in hindsight, but that's not how we saw it. I had a Boston poster (the band, not the city), a Randy Rhoads one I bought after he died—it had his birth and death dates at the bottom: DECEMBER 6TH, 1956 – MARCH 19TH, 1982. That stuck with me because my birthday is December 7. And of course, there was Heather Thomas in a pink bikini. She was my favorite—even more than the Agree bottle. Back then, there were two Heathers: you were either Team Thomas or Team Locklear. No contest.

I also had clippings from *Hit Parader, Kerrang!,* and *Circus* maga-
zines—Joe Elliott, Eddie Van Halen, Alex Lifeson—and a giant KISS
poster with their faces stacked *Brady Bunch* style. Hard rock royalty,
all over my walls.

There was a kerosene heater next to my bed because the basement got
cold. I always thought it was going to blow up and kill us all. But it
was the '70s—nobody thought that kind of stuff through.
Except me.

Oh shit—I almost forgot the black-light posters. Those were mint. I
was the only one of my friends who had them. Three in a row, right
over my bed, with a black light hanging above. One had a white tiger,
one was a weird psychedelic pattern that looked like it moved if you
squinted, and the third? No clue—it's blank in my brain. I also had
one of those standing tree lights with three adjustable sockets. One
regular bulb, two red. Very "budget vampire decor."

And then—*the* lava lamp. Courtesy of Spencer's. Blue light, white
wax. That lava lamp would follow me to college and probably has
more stories to tell than I'd care to put in these pages.

The whole space was less of a bedroom and more like a lair.

It was the perfect setup for the way I liked to drink at the time. I'd
turn on the red light and the black light to set the mood. My vibe was
one part romantic, one part melancholy, and one part self-pity. Next
came the music. I had a rotation of depressing albums that enhanced
the dark vibes: *The Head on the Door* by The Cure, *Black Celebration*
by Depeche Mode, and *The Queen Is Dead* by The Smiths. Chef's
kiss.

Then I'd pour myself a wine cooler, take out my journal, and write
poetry. It was always sad. I was a fucking excellent writer back then. It
was the only subject in school I both enjoyed and excelled at. My
stuff was always dark—lost love, being broken, and for some reason...
war.

At sixteen, I was already romancing alcohol. I aspired to be like Charles Bukowski or Hemingway—both of whom drank themselves into oblivion, by the way. That's probably when I crossed the line from weekend partier to someone teetering between angsty teenager and full-blown alcoholic. Drinking by myself became something I liked way more than drinking socially. I never shared that with anyone. Not even my friends. I knew it wasn't a good thing, but in a morbid way, I fed off the misery it conjured. I was never good at flipping a switch to be happy. I couldn't control how long I stayed happy. But man, could I control my misery. I was a master at it.

I was starting to spiral and had no idea where it would eventually lead me.

Not long ago, I was cleaning out some boxes of nostalgia and found an old journal full of poems I'd written—tiny emotional grenades I'd lobbed onto the page because I didn't know how else to be heard.

### NEGLECTED (written in 1986)

*Why all the anger? Why the despair?*
*I'm led to believe that nobody cared.*
*When you were young, did you ever smile?*
*Or were you deprived of life as a child?*
*Whatever the reason, why ever the pain,*
*Stop living this lie you try to restrain.*

My drinking continued to spiral. On the outside, my friends saw me as a happy, funny drunk. I was also the chief enabler—the guy who encouraged everyone else to drink, even if they didn't want to. I wanted everyone to *want* to drink as much as I did. I needed them to *need* to drink as much as I did.

The more I drank, the less I felt.

I had never dealt with my parents' divorce or what it did to me. I know now that I experienced a level of trauma that totally warped the way I saw the world. From a young age, I collected resentments like some people collect baseball cards—flipping through them, memorizing the stats, holding on to them like they'll be worth something one day. I had no idea they'd become the currency of my self-destruction.

And that part of me—the one stuffed full of silence, anger, and unfinished grief—started to surface more and more.

Especially when I met Leigh.

# I Don't Have Horns, but I am Horny

I continued to drink alone regularly throughout high school. It finally surfaced as a problem in my senior year. I had a new girlfriend that I met in homeroom. Her name was Leigh. She was really hot. Blond hair, blue eyes and a smokin' hot body. She moved to the neighborhood from Tennessee of all places. We sat right next to each other. I was really nice to her. I definitely turned on the charm. She would have normally been way out of my league, but she was fresh meat and none the wiser. I hit the jackpot with her. She knew nothing about me except that I had a varsity wrestling jacket and I was funny.

It was almost too good to be true. I made sure to close the deal quickly. She was adorable. She liked hard rock, and she had this quiet edge to her.

All I knew about her was that she had a serious boyfriend back in Tennessee who did hard drugs and was supposedly a headcase. Not a problem. No one in my immediate circle did any drugs. I definitely didn't. Drugs scared the shit out of me. Sports were always a huge part of my childhood, so smoking cigarettes or pot was never on the table. Only the dirtbags did that shit.

Drugs were a line in the sand I swore I would never cross. Eventually I wouldn't just cross it, I would drive over it with a fifteen-foot tall Monster Truck decked out with seventy-inch tires, nitrogen-charged shocks, supercharged engine, and a pair of oversized fuzzy dice hanging from the rearview.

Most importantly, Leigh was down to drink and fool around. She had way more experience than I did when it came to sex. I had gotten a couple of amateur hand jobs at the low-rent Jewish summer camp I went to when I was thirteen, and I had fooled around with a bunch of girls throughout high school, but I was still a virgin. I lied and told her I wasn't because I had a clean slate with her, so why not?

I remember when she found out I was Jewish; she admitted she had never met a Jewish person before. When I met her mother for the first time, she asked me if I wore a hat to hide my horns. I had no fucking clue what she was talking about, so I just laughed it off and changed the subject. When I got home later that day and asked my mom what she meant, she just about lost her latkes. That was some real antisemitic rhetoric to throw out there in the middle of Long Island. Holy hell. Had her parents not done their research? New York is literally the most Jewish place in the world aside from Israel. You can't spit without hitting a synagogue. I'm also pretty sure her dad hated me. Every time I walked through the door he would throw me the stink eye from his La-Z-Boy. I don't think he gave a shit about the whole Jewish thing. I don't think he even cared that I was schtupping his daughter. I do think he suspected I was stealing his beer, though. Under any other circumstances I would have hightailed my ass out of there, but getting laid was way too important to worry about a mild case of Judeophobia. Nothing to see here.

Man, that was an awesome time. I'm pretty sure I lost my virginity while listening to Guns N' Roses for the first time. Between her and the beer, I was pretty much uninterested in anything else. I had just finished my last wrestling season as a co-captain of the team. I was coasting through the second half of my senior year, and my drinking was getting progressively worse. I would rendezvous with my girlfriend every day at her house during school hours, we'd have sex, I'd grab a few of her dad's beers from the fridge, and then I'd put on my Ray-Bans and stumble back to class. I'd hide behind those sunglasses and a heavy buzz for the remainder of the school year.

My teachers started to notice, and most of all, Leigh became concerned.

I was volatile and angry most of the time, and when I drank, I got belligerent. I never hit anyone, but I had a real talent for breaking windows, shattering glass, and punching holes in walls. I was reckless. And let's be honest—there's nothing scarier than a rogue white Jew-boy from Long Island.

One time, my mother approached me. She'd found all of the beer and wine coolers that she had purchased the day before, but they were empty. She asked me where they all went, and I told her that my friends and I had drunk them all. Sensing that I was drunk at the time, she called bullshit. I lost my cool and ran out of the house. It was pouring rain, and I walked a few miles toward my girlfriend's house. By coincidence, she was on her way to me and spotted me on the road. She pulled over and picked me up.

This was probably the first time I thought to myself that I might have a problem with alcohol. Leigh's mother, who was extremely Christian and worked at the school, suggested I get help. Being seventeen, I wasn't quite sure what that meant, so I tried to manage it on my own.

I would eventually distance myself from them both. This was something that had become quite common. Pulling away from the people I loved most was second nature. I wasn't good at being vulnerable. I was never honest, and I wasn't going to let anybody disappoint me like my mom and dad did when they got divorced. Letting people in was not an option, especially ones who wanted to help.

I didn't know it then, but I was already writing about dependence—just not on the alcohol yet. This is a poem I wrote about her in 1988. It wasn't just about her. It was about what I thought love was supposed to save me from.

## Leigh

*I think of you forever in the moments we're apart.*
*The minutes stretch in silence—they tear inside my heart.*
*In visions I can touch you, you lay here by my side,*
*You wipe away the tears of loneliness I've cried.*
*My heart now runs on empty. I think of you each day.*
*Your shadow I will follow. I long for you to stay.*
*Don't leave me here in darkness, a bottle in my arms—*
*Appreciate my love for you, and shield me from all harm.*
*My only link to lifetime grows weaker every day,*
*But since you're there to rescue me, our love won't fade away.*

My thoughts were getting darker, and it showed in my writing. I wasn't suicidal, but the line between my thoughts and reality was starting to blur. That poem wasn't just about Leigh—it was about the fantasy that someone, anyone, could save me from myself.

The truth is, there *was* love in my life. Real love. I didn't know how to let it in. But it was there all along.

# Mother of the Year

I didn't know how to talk to my mom. Not about real things. Not about how I was doing, or how I was feeling, or why I kept pretending none of it affected me. I didn't have the language for that —not in high school, not in any school, really.

What I did know how to do was act out. I knew how to scream and yell, how to punch holes in the wall, how to disappear behind a closed bedroom door and blast heavy metal that said everything I didn't. I knew how to make her feel like she wasn't getting it right, even when she was doing her absolute best just to keep it all from going to absolute shit.

Looking back, I can only imagine how powerless she must have felt. Trying to reach a son who wouldn't speak. A son who had learned how to build walls quicker than he could tie his shoes. I think she wanted a close relationship with me more than anything in the world —but I didn't know how to give it to her. I don't think I even knew what it was supposed to look like.

Maybe I just didn't know how to trust love that didn't walk out. My dad left. She didn't. But I still kept her at arm's length. Maybe I blamed her for sticking around when everything else was falling apart. Maybe I thought that if I let her in, she'd leave too—and it would hurt worse because I actually needed her. I don't know. I just know she kept showing up, and I kept shutting the door.

She still tells me today that she never really knew what I was feeling when I was a kid. That she'd always wished I would open up more. I hear the guilt in her voice when she says it—even now, even after all these years and all the healing we've done. She wonders what she missed. I wonder what I buried. Neither of us has the full story.

And I get it. Because deep down, I was carrying guilt, too. Not for the divorce—that was never mine to carry—but for how I treated her in the aftermath. She'd been the only parent still standing, and I'd made her pay for both of them.

I think that's why I did it.

That's why I entered her into the Mother of the Year contest.

It was one of those small-town newspaper things. All you had to do was write an essay explaining why your mom deserved it. The prize was a bunch of gift certificates to every store in town, and your mom's photo in the paper. I didn't tell her I was doing it. I didn't ask for help or feedback. I just sat down, sixteen years old, full of feelings I didn't know how to say—and wrote this:

*Dear Judges,*

*My name is Jason Mayo and I am a student at Mill Creek High School. I'm sixteen years old and I think my mother is super. Maybe I should rephrase that to "Superwoman." Most letters you have read in the past have probably been typical writings from those who love their mother—just as I do. But I think this mother is deservant of a superior honor such as your Mother of the Year.*

*My mother is different. My parents have been divorced for almost eight years now, and it took me this long until I could appreciate what she has done for my brother and me in the past and present.*

*Throughout her motherhood, she has cared for us in the kindest way and helped to round our character in the finest way possible. She works very hard as a teacher in Queens, and she puts forth an incredible effort in her profession. She is also attending school in order to get various credits for her higher degree.*

*Besides working and going to school, she is a friend above friends to those that she cares for.*

*It's hard to describe the strength she possesses within by just describing her actions. She not only accepts and succeeds at her title of mother, but she must at times be there as a father because we are at home a family of three.*

*She amazes me with her spirited personality and her deep philosophy. Many a time she could have quit on us because we've seen not only good times but bad. But it's that strong-hearted character that keeps our family not a family of three, but a family of three together as one.*

*I cannot imagine another person as qualified for this honor you offer. It's hard for me to tell her how special she is to us and how thankful we are for her guidance, but I thought you could help me by presenting her with a title as rewarding as that of Mother of the Year.*

*It's my turn to make her smile. She's been waiting for a long time. I love her.*

*Yours Truly,*

*Jason Mayo*

. . .

And I meant every word. I just didn't know how to say it to her out loud.

But I did write one more thing. A poem. Just a few lines—nothing fancy. But it was mine. And it was hers. And I think now, looking back, it was maybe the most emotionally honest thing I wrote at that age:

### My Mother

*Always ready to judge you fair,*
*To me your sorrows I can share.*
*Just chance on me, I'll help you fight,*
*For you can come be day or night.*
*With soothing smile and open arms,*
*I feel your pain and shield your harms.*
*I don't want much by ways of gold,*
*Just to find your warmth when I am cold.*
*To die for you may be extreme—*
*I live for you though, it may seem.*
*In times of need when teardrops fall,*
*I will be there to heed your call.*

Her reaction when she found out she'd won? Pure joy—and complete surprise. There was no "cool" in that moment. No distance. No sarcasm. Just my mom glowing. Laughing. Smiling bigger than I'd seen in years. She got her picture in the paper. She got her prizes. But more than that, I think—for a second—she felt seen.

And for a second, I think I felt a little less broken.

We have a good relationship today. Not a sitcom-ending one. But solid. Real. She still wants to know what I'm feeling, and I still don't always know how to say it. But I say it more than I used to. And she listens. And that's something.

Healing's a lifelong process. Sometimes it looks like therapy and long conversations. Sometimes it looks like forgiveness. And sometimes it looks like a teenager, scared and angry and full of love he doesn't know how to express, writing a secret letter to remind the world just how lucky he is to have his mom in it.

And there were other anchors in my life—people who helped carry the weight without ever needing credit. Even if I didn't realize it yet.

# Tanqueray and Tenderness
# (Lightly Stirred)

I have really fond memories of my extended family, especially my grandparents. Even before my parents split up, I adored them all. They were wildly different from one another in personality and upbringing, but they had one very important thing in common: they loved the hell out of me and my brother. After my dad left, going to my grandparents' homes felt like entering a safe zone. No matter what chaos was unraveling between my mom and dad, my grandparents made sure none of it reached us. Their homes were soft landings —predictable, peaceful, full of warmth and normalcy. No yelling. No bad-mouthing. No tension. Just cookies, games, and tons of food.

But I didn't have to look very far to figure out that my love affair with alcohol was rooted deep in the family tree. Honestly, it wasn't just one branch—it was the whole damn canopy. Both sides of my family were Eastern European stock, so I was a mutt: part Russian, part German, part Polish. Nostrovia. Oktoberfest. Pierogi. I never had a chance.

**Dad's Side**

My clearest memories of my dad's parents are surprisingly simple. I'd sit in the kitchen with my Nana while she drank tea and I inhaled Stella D'oro Swiss Fudge cookies—the round, floral-shaped ones with the chocolate dollop in the center. She always had those and the breakfast treats, perfect for dunking. She loved playing Rummikub. I can still hear the clack of the tiles as she poured them out onto the table. I didn't care if I won or lost—I just loved being there. I felt safe. I could exhale.

She also loved *The Rockford Files*. James Garner was like Ryan Gosling for old people—so fucking cool. Great hair, the perfect amount of swagger. That theme song still lives in my head rent free—the answering machine message and all. Nana had this green leather swivel chair that made fart sounds when you moved in it, which was hilarious for reasons I refuse to outgrow.

They'd put my brother to bed first, and then she and I would stay up and watch *Rockford*. I felt like a big kid. Not the "little man" I was expected to be at home—just a kid with special privileges for a night. I miss them.

## Mom's Side

My first drink was probably with my maternal grandfather. He was small in build but tough as nails. Not the emotional or lovey-dovey type. He fought in the Polish army during World War II and lost almost his entire family in the Holocaust—so yeah, he got a pass.

I *loved* going to their house. Their home felt different—sacred, almost. My mom's parents were more traditional, a little religious. They kept kosher and had Shabbat dinner every Friday. It wasn't fancy, just proper. And deeply loving.

My grandpa had a seltzer truck business called Sid's Seltzer, so they had all these amazing glass seltzer bottles with metal nozzles. And his egg creams? Forget it. You haven't lived until you've had an egg cream made by a Polish Jew who knows what he's doing. Everything in that house was homemade—egg creams, jams, cakes, soups. They even made their own pickles. My grandma cooked breakfast, lunch, and dinner like it was a full-time job—*and* she had a full-time job. She commuted into the city five days a week, walking fifteen blocks to her office. She did that until she was seventy-five. The woman was a machine.

She was also a Holocaust survivor. She'd been in a concentration camp as a young girl. So yeah, she didn't waste a drop of anything. Gratitude wasn't a concept in that house—it was just baked into the way they lived.

Their backyard was like a damn farm. Tomatoes the size of grapefruits, cucumbers, peppers, radishes—you name it. Grape vines, blueberry bushes, strawberries, flowers everywhere. They even had one of those round above-ground pools that felt Olympic-size back then. Everything about that house was a time capsule. The furniture looked imported from the old country, all handmade. They spoke Yiddish unless they were speaking to us. The whole language sounded like one long sneeze—but it was beautiful. A blend of German, Hebrew, Slavic, and 100 percent chutzpah.

**The First Sip**

When I was a kid, drinking always seemed fun—*celebratory*. Especially in that house. Everyone seemed lighter with a drink in hand. But it wasn't just the alcohol—it was the *ritual*. The cabinet. The glassware. The sparkle.

My grandpa *loved* making drinks. He had this beautiful cabinet in the living room that opened up into a lit-up bar full of gleaming bottles and fancy glasses. Most of it was old people booze—blackberry brandy, schnapps, crème de cassis, Manischewitz, Kahlúa. But one bottle stood above the rest: a giant emerald bottle of Tanqueray gin.

He pushed that stuff like a nomad selling water in the desert. Every guest got offered a gin and tonic in his thick Polish accent. But it wasn't just any gin and tonic—it was *his* recipe. Three parts gin, one part tonic, a splash of grenadine, and a maraschino cherry. Always a cherry.

That was probably my very first encounter with alcohol. I was around nine, right after my parents split up, right when everything felt uncertain. My grandpa snuck me a sip—nothing dramatic, just a small taste, probably when my grandma wasn't looking. She would've pulled him by the ear if she knew.

But that made it even *cooler.*

He made me feel worthy of the thing adults treated like treasure. And I remember that first sip like it was yesterday. Gin on its own is rough. Tonic? Basically carbonated pine needle piss. But together— with grenadine and that gloriously synthetic cherry—it felt like magic.

From that moment on, I *romanticized* alcohol. I never saw it as dangerous. Only as something happy, something shared, something adult and special. A privilege. Big person medicine. And I *wanted* that.

Every visit after that my grandpa would pour me a gin and tonic. Over the years, the ritual stayed, even as he started to fade. Near the end, his bartending skills got shaky. The gin became vodka, the tonic became seltzer, and eventually, every bottle in the cabinet found its way into the glass. It was basically turpentine. But I drank it anyway. I didn't have the heart to tell him. I just sipped and let him enjoy me enjoying it.

Looking back now, my grandpa was probably my first drinking buddy.

If I could've frozen that time—and everything alcohol meant to me in that moment—I would have. But that was only the beginning.

My grandpa might have opened the door, but it wasn't long before I learned how to tear it off the hinges.

# Cool Cousins and the Cocaine Bus

E very summer, my dad's side of the family would pile onto a coach bus and make an annual pilgrimage to upstate New York. His side was *huge*. The exact opposite of my mom's family. Loud, chaotic, wild—in the best way.

My grandpa had a bunch of siblings, they had a bunch of kids, and they all had a bunch of kids. And everyone was tight. They all grew up in Brooklyn. Not today's Brooklyn with gluten-free, vegan, ironic mustache, goldendoodle-flannel energy. I'm talking street stickball, mom-and-pop hardware stores, open fire hydrants, cops with billy clubs, and Sandy Fucking Koufax. Back when "family" wasn't just who lived in your house—it was the whole damn block.

Whenever I got to hang with my dad's family, it was a *trip*. I had about six or seven older cousins, and I looked up to every single one of them. They were ten to fifteen years older—already drinking, smoking, getting laid, going to concerts, working jobs, obsessed with the Mets. They were the older brothers I never had. In my own world, I had no real direction and no real example to follow. So when they let me in, made me feel cool, let me curse and talk shit and included me in their conversations—I *lived* for that.

When summer hit, I counted the days to the family outing. It was only a single day, but it felt like a week every time. We packed so much fun into it, and the bus ride was always my favorite part.

The younger generation (mostly in their late twenties) loaded coolers with Budweiser and ice. The old-timers came armed with mini briefcases packed with flasks, shakers, and tumblers. Inside: scotch, gin, vodka. It was all very Rat Pack.

I learned how to drink *properly* on that bus. There was a whole unspoken system. By the time I was thirteen, I was drinking cold beers with the crew like I was on a lunch break at a construction site. That family could *drink*. There were times we should've been facedown in a ditch before we even got there. But by the time we pulled up, everyone was lit up like fireflies—and it was only 10 a.m.

By midday we were playing wiffle ball and smoking pot. I didn't touch drugs at first—I was just happy drinking and being included. I think they liked having me around. I was young, but not so young that I ruined the vibe. Maybe they felt sorry for me, too. My dad's family *loved* my mom, so even when she wasn't there, they always asked about her. To be honest, I got the sense they were still pissed at him for leaving us. Even in a family that wild, we were the only broken home. And I always felt it.

While we were doing our thing, the older adults would wander off to play cards and drink. The men smoked cigars, cracked jokes, and argued about baseball. Everyone was a character. My grandpa's brother—my great-uncle—was simply called Mayo. That was our last name. I still don't even know his first name. He was like an old Jewish Sting. Just Mayo.

He always got the drunkest the fastest. He was a born entertainer, a one-man vaudeville act. He'd mess up his hair, act like a lunatic, and sing in made-up Spanish until people lost it. He always managed to find a piano, too. I don't think he actually knew how to play, but he definitely knew how to *perform*. When he died, I remember the old-timers hanging back at the gravesite after everyone else had left. They passed around a flask, took a sip, and poured a little into the dirt. It was *baller*.

In my family, alcohol wasn't just something people did—it was the *thread*. It connected everyone. I picked up on that early.

Sometimes after lunch, my dad would break off with me and my brother to hit tennis balls around. Some of my best memories with him were out there on the court. He'd pretend my serve was 100 miles an hour, even when I hit the net every time. And we'd laugh like idiots whenever I launched the ball over the fence. He'd toss out little tips—how to hold the racket, how to follow through—just enough to make it feel like we were doing something real. In those moments, we almost felt like a real father and son. But just for the weekend. Then I'd turn back into a pumpkin.

He wasn't a big sports guy—except for tennis. It was always *tennis, tennis, tennis*. He loved Jimmy Connors. Back then, tennis players were like rockstars. Total maniacs. Screaming at umpires, whipping rackets across the court like Chinese stars. It was half sport, half performance art. I hated tennis, but even I had to admit—it was kind of badass back then.

I don't remember what we ate—maybe packed sandwiches, maybe catered food. We usually went to one of those Catskills resort-type places, like a busted *Dirty Dancing* set. Half the time I wasn't even sure we were supposed to be there. We might've been trespassing for all I knew. Wouldn't have surprised me.

The summer before I left for college, I was *ready* for that outing. I had a steady girlfriend, I wasn't a virgin anymore, and I was captain of the wrestling team. I was drinking regularly by then and couldn't wait to party with my cousins. I wasn't just the little cousin anymore —I was one of the guys.

That year, I pushed to play real softball instead of just wiffle ball. We had the people, we had the gear, and we found a field nearby we could use. Everyone was down. We loaded up the gloves, bats, balls, beer, and piled back onto the bus to drive over.

I was pumped. I was good at softball—fast, good glove, decent power. My cousins were competitive, too, but looking back, none of them were exactly athletes. I used to think they were amazing at everything, but now I realize... they were pretty mid. It was kind of hilarious.

By game time, we were already three sheets to the wind. I had smoked pot for the first time earlier that year, so I was ready to flex that skill, too. I was pulling out all the stops. And it was going *great*. I was easily the best player on the field.

About halfway through the game, my team was up to bat. I was on deck, hyped to smash another shot. One of my older cousins—the one I was closest to—called me over to the bus. I figured he was handing me a beer, maybe giving me an on-deck pep talk.

Instead, he pulled me onto the bus and told me to sit down. He pulled out a bag of something that definitely wasn't weed.

"You ever tried coke?" he asked.

I thought, *Dude, I just turned seventeen. It's my second summer with pubes. You're like thirty. What do you think?*

But he didn't wait for an answer.

He told me he knew I was going to college soon, and he wanted me to try the hard stuff with *him*—so I'd be safe. Real older brother energy, except instead of giving me condoms or life advice, he gave me a rolled-up dollar bill and a line cut on the armrest of a bus seat.

My dad and the rest of the family were maybe fifty feet away. I didn't even hesitate. That's the part that gets me now—it wasn't scary. It wasn't taboo. It felt like he was handing me a piece of grape Bubble Yum and asking if I'd ever tried that flavor before.

Winner, winner, chicken dinner.

It was different. The buzz hit *fast*—the beer, the pot, and now the coke all crashing together like some teenage Hunter S. Thompson starter pack.

Then I heard my dad call me—it was my turn at bat.

I stepped up to the plate, wired out of my skull, and launched the first pitch over the centerfield fence like I was Darryl Strawberry in a Bar Mitzvah League. I probably ran those bases like my ass was on fire, grinning like I'd won the lottery. No one suspected a thing.

I was off to the races—literally and figuratively.

I was ready for college.

*Thanks, cuz.*

I think I crossed a line that day—and not just the one on the armrest. It didn't feel like a turning point. It felt like tradition. A weird, messed up, chemically enhanced rite of passage, handed down with a wink and a half-empty beer. I wasn't just getting high. I was preparing for the Ivy League of self-sabotage. So, naturally, I chose a school with more bars than classrooms and a student body that treated partying like an extracurricular.

# Part Two
# I'm Fucked

# I Want You to Want Me

My relationship with my dad was complicated. Most of what I've written about him in this book isn't flattering—and not because I set out to make him a villain. It's just where the pain lived. I resented him for a long time. Before I even knew what a resentment was, I just knew I was angry. I blamed him. I was disappointed.

But that doesn't mean I didn't love him. Quite the opposite.

I wanted so badly to connect with him—to trust him, to feel unconditionally loved by him. But that's hard to do when you have to drive seventy-five miles across two bridges just to see someone. As much as I dreaded going to his place, there was always a part of me that *wanted* to want to be there.

And I think—despite the distance, the silence, the awkward weekends—he craved love from me, too. I didn't fully understand that until I became a father myself. There's a bond between a parent and a kid that's unbreakable. Almost impossible to explain. And I can't imagine he didn't carry guilt for not being there more. Whatever happened between him and my mom was beside the point.

After Connecticut, my dad and Dominique moved to New Jersey—probably the smelliest place on the planet. I remember sitting in bumper-to-bumper traffic on the Belt Parkway, crawling toward the Verrazzano, dreading what I knew was coming. As soon as we crossed the Goethals Bridge, it hit like a brick wall: the smell of garbage and chemicals swirling together in the air, like someone was trying to cook spoiled meat on a tire fire. The smokestacks belched out plumes of who-the-hell-knows-what, exhaling chemicals into the sky like they were rewriting the atmosphere one toxic sigh at a time—single-handedly destroying the planet. And yet... it was our destination. Scotch Plains, New Jersey. Smelled like hell, but it had my dad.

By that point, he'd upgraded from the green Datsun B210 to a yellow Nissan Stanza XE with brown trim—proof that automotive progress didn't always mean aesthetic progress. The thing looked like it had been dipped in expired mustard and trimmed in corduroy. Still, I was relieved. The B210 had about as much legroom as the hyperbaric chamber from *Altered States*. At least now I could stretch out.

It was a stick shift, and I was instantly obsessed. My dad made it look so easy, and he knew I wanted in on the action, so he let me shift the gears. The diagram was right there on the knob, and I'd sit there like a puppy waiting for cues...

"Now?"

"Not yet."

"Now?"

"Not yet."

"Okay—first!"

"Now?"

"Second!"

"Now?"

"Third!"

I would've done it the whole way if he'd let me.

He always played music. Always. He had a stack of cassettes in the car, but I only wanted one: the one that kicked off with "I Want You to Want Me"—the *At Budokan* version, of course. That Rick Nielsen riff hit like a starter pistol. We couldn't start the trip without it.

Peaches & Herb's "Reunited" was on that tape too—irony totally lost on me at the time, though now it makes me laugh and cry in equal measure. "Stumblin' In." "Sad Eyes." One of those K-Tel greatest hits compilations from '79 or '80. God, I'd give my left arm to crank that tape in the truck with my kids now.

Getting to his place always felt a little off. Especially at first. Our room didn't have much of us in it. We'd pull out the bed, set everything up, and yeah—Dominique would change the "shits."

Looking back, they could've at least slapped a poster on the wall— Farrah Fawcett, maybe, or that Boston one with the flying guitar.

But instead? A collection of French porcelain dolls, perched like they were guarding some cursed family secret. All of them staring, wide-eyed and dead inside, like they'd kill me in my sleep if their tiny limbs weren't so brittle.

Still, he always told me to bring my baseball mitt. He couldn't make many of my Little League games, but one thing we always did was play catch. Always on the side of the townhouse development. No big yard. Just a little patch of grass at the end. He'd feed me grounders, then launch a pop-up like he was trying to take down a satellite.

I'd pitch to him, too. He'd squat down like a catcher and pretend to call signals. I'd shake them off until I got the one I liked—even though I only knew how to throw one pitch, a fastball that maybe hit 30 MPH if I had a tailwind. Still, he'd pull his hand out of his glove and shake it like I was throwing heat like the Goose.

There was a train that passed right behind his townhouse—ten feet from the back wall. It wasn't a passenger train, just a long, loud freight line that clattered by a few times a day. I loved it. We'd pause whatever we were doing and watch the whole thing go by. Each car a moment. Each car a breath.

But the best part of visiting my dad?

The music.

His vinyl collection was insane. There must've been at least a hundred albums, pristine and alphabetized. He cleaned each one before playing it—something I still do to this day. His stereo system was no joke. Looked like a server rack at IBM. Huge receiver, just the right mix of analog dials and digital readouts. Auto-drop turntable. Speakers that looked like pillars. Giant gray-and-blue headphones that felt like two memory foam pillows on your head.

That's how I discovered Steely Dan, Stevie Wonder, Clapton, Rod Stewart, and yeah—even Barbra Streisand. My dad was obsessed with her. You'd think if he loved her any more, he would've skipped Dominique and just married Babs instead. I never liked her much, but that *Guilty* album with Barry Gibb? Perfection.


And then there were Sunday mornings.

That was when my dad became the self-proclaimed "Breakfast Man." The guy could barbecue, sure—but breakfast was where he really flexed. We'd wake up to the smell of bacon and the sound of Neil Diamond roaring through the speakers. My dad belting it out, gravelly voiced and glorious, while I sang backup in my footed pajamas. He had every album and knew every word. If he had owned a sequined jumpsuit, he would've worn it.

Dominique would shout from upstairs for us to turn it down—but he never did. Not that time.

"I Am... I Said" was our church. And pancakes, our communion.

He stacked them high and threw two sunny-side-up eggs on top so the yolks spilled over like lava. Neil in the background. It was loud. It was ridiculous. It was perfect.

Looking back now, I wonder what it would've been like if my parents hadn't split. Would it have always been like that—catch, pancakes, and Neil? Or was he just trying to cram a lifetime's worth of fatherhood into forty-eight hours?

As an adult, I swore I would never be like my dad. I'd never abandon my family. Never blow up my life. I clung so hard to that vow, I sometimes missed the point—I focused more on *not* destroying my relationships than actually trying to make them work. I was trying so hard not to fail like him, I didn't realize how complicated things can get. How much gray lives between right and wrong. Between leaving and staying.

No one goes into something hoping to fail. But sometimes it happens.

I like to think I took the best of us with me—

The Saturday morning playlists.

The pancakes and bacon.

The off-key singing that makes my kids groan.

The rhythm of a gear shift.

The glove that still held the shape of my hand—and maybe his, too.

That's the part that stuck.

There's one thing I always remember about my dad—back then, and even now: the way he hugged me when he picked us up, and when he dropped us off. The kiss on the cheek that smacked a little. The kind that lasts just a beat too long, but not long enough. The one that came with an "I love you" whispered in my ear.

In those moments, I felt loved. I felt like his son. I felt—maybe—like I was enough.

Then I'd watch him vanish into the driver's seat of that yellow Nissan Stanza, gears grinding like a protest, and the last echoes of Cheap Trick swallowed by the dark.

And just like that, I was back to being the kid with divorced parents. The kid who wanted to disappear. The kid who never stopped wanting to be wanted.

# Frat Houses, Fast Eddie, and DJ Jazzy Jeff

I honestly have no memory of applying to colleges, but somehow I ended up at the State University of New York at Oneonta—about four hours from home, in the middle of upstate nowhere. I knew exactly three things about it going in. First, it was nicknamed "Stoneonta." Second, it was a teaching school with a four-to-one girl-to-guy ratio. And third—and most important—Oneonta had more bars per square mile than any other college town in the country. Jackpot.

It was the perfect breeding ground for my drinking: I was seventeen, away from home, and completely anonymous. A clean slate, and I couldn't wait to fuck it up.

My freshman year in college, I roomed with my buddy Paul from high school. He was about six foot four, drove a Ford Bronco and loved to drink. We made sure our room was stocked with cases of Milwaukee's Best and cheap bottles of vodka. A case of MB was about $5. It tasted like toilet water, but it did the trick.

I was drinking pretty much every day, and it was a beautiful thing. I pledged a fraternity and found myself surrounded by alcohol and drugs. It was everywhere, and it was easy to find. My funny guy, partying nature, continued to evolve, and my volatility got worse. There were more broken windows and punching walls, and now I was even getting into fistfights. I was addicted to the adrenaline rush of it all and began to get a reputation as a bit of a lunatic. I wasn't the biggest guy out there, but I had no problem scrapping with anyone, especially when I was drunk.

I never said no during my four years of college. I went to every party, smoked every bong hit, did every mushroom, and snorted every line. Being high was easy. Being sober was hard. All the while, I was making more and more friends, but at the same time, I continued to push the people who loved me further and further away. I was the guy who was friends with everyone but really had no one. It was a lonely existence for me on the inside.

My dad liked to party, and every once in a while, he'd show up at school to visit. Everyone loved it when he came—including me. He'd drink and smoke with us, and people would always tell me how jealous they were of how close we were. I thought I was lucky at the time, but now I realize that partying together was the only way my dad and I could communicate. We never talked about anything serious, and we never talked about our feelings or how much I was hurting because he left when I was so young. He didn't seem so concerned about my alcohol and drug use. Or that their money was being funneled into keg parties and dime bags instead of textbooks.

My dad would come to visit with his best friend Eddie every once in a while. Eddie was awesome. He was funny as hell. Really dry sense of humor. A great straight man for my dad—an Abbott to my dad's Costello. They looked so much alike that people always assumed they were brothers. They might as well have been. They would party with us every step of the way. Although once in a while my dad would disappear without warning, and we'd later find him passed out in my room, fully clothed, listening to Pink Floyd with a half-smoked joint on the night table. They would also pay for everything when they came up. My friends loved them. They gave them the nicknames Fast Eddie and DJ Jazzy Jeff. They were legends. When I look back, I have a hard time believing that my dad was only in his mid-forties. I'm in my fifties now. Crazy.

There was one time that my dad came to visit for the weekend and I decided to prank him. That semester, weed was passe' and hash oil was the drug du jour. This was back in the late '80s and the crack epidemic was in full swing. In order to smoke the hash oil, we would put some on a piece of aluminum foil, light it from underneath and inhale the smoke through a straw. To the layman's eye, it looked exactly like we were smoking crack. I knew my dad would want to smoke with us when he got there, so I convinced my friends to pretend we were smoking crack instead of hash oil. I wanted to see if my dad would actually agree to smoke crack with his son at college. It took about a minute for me to persuade him to do it. My friends almost pissed themselves. That was a father of the year moment for sure.

The drinking remained constant. I even had a run-in with the local police for driving drunk. I remember specifically a time when a friend and I went drinking. We started out relatively early in the day. There was a happy-hour special called "Beat the Clock" at a local pub that we loved to hang out at. There was usually a mellow crowd, and it was a bit out of the way. We drove there in my friend's beat-up station wagon. It looked like the Family Truckster from *National Lampoon's Vacation*.

The concept was simple: drinks started at $1. Every half hour, drinks would go up a quarter. There was no limit. Shots, beer, wine—everything was fair game. We probably hung out and drank for five hours before we decided to head back to campus. Clearly, we were wasted. Neither of us could walk straight. My friend looked at me and conceded that there was no way he could possibly drive. Without hesitation, I assured him that I had it under control.

We got in the car, with me behind the wheel of the Family Truck-ster, and we drove off. We made it about half a mile before we decided we needed to stop for some heroes. There was a gas station/food mart just up the road. When I pulled in, I overshot the island with the gas tanks by about three feet. I hopped the island, and the side of the car scraped loudly across the side of one of the gas tanks.

My friend was furious—not because I nearly blew up half the town, but because I had dinged the shittiest-looking vehicle in history. I laughed, bought us two heroes, and that seemed to settle it. Appar-ently sandwiches > explosions. Then, like idiots, we both got back in the car.

Unbeknownst to me, a cop car had followed us all the way back to campus. I'm not sure if he'd seen me jump the island at the gas station, but regardless, he'd picked up on my erratic driving. He pulled me over on campus about fifteen yards away from my dorm parking spot.

He walked over to us and asked that I get out of the car. He then asked if I had been drinking. I said that I had not been drinking. He put me through all the various tests: reciting the alphabet, walking a straight line, and even directing me to touch my fingers to my nose. I specifically remember seeing double while trying to walk in a straight line.

This had to be the end of my run. I was going to go to jail. People would be disappointed in me. I was fucked.

The cop then asked me where I was going. I pointed to the parking spot just off to the left. He looked me in the eye and said, "Park your car, and if I ever pull you over again, you're gonna be sorry."

That was it. No ticket. No jail. Holy shit. I'd gotten off scot-free. I was always great at talking my way out of things. I was pretty good at lying. It's easy to lie when you believe it yourself...

Over the next few years, I focused mainly on drinking and smoking pot—occasionally throwing in a mushroom or two, until I ran into a brick wall face-first because I mistook it for a pile of snakes. I put in the minimal effort it took to pass my classes. I was active in my fraternity, played sports, and even started working as a DJ at the school radio station. On the outside, everything looked great. But on the inside, I was hurting.

I still loved to drink alone. Whether it was Bloody Marys and bacon, egg, and cheese for breakfast while reading the paper, or a few beers at night while listening to music, it was something I did to relax. I'd have to say that it was in the last two years of college that I began to consciously become aware of my isolation techniques.

Falling head over heels for a girl and then, months later, pushing her away became common. I'd tell myself that I hadn't found the right girl yet, but I knew something wasn't right. After my breakup, I'd isolate myself even more, and the drinking became heavier. I'd wallow in self-pity and drown my sorrows in booze and weed.

I wasn't comfortable unless I was numb.

More and more, alcohol was becoming my crutch. Stressed out because of a test? A few beers would take the edge off. Celebrating a win on the football field? Let's get smashed until we can't stand. Whatever the situation, I had begun to live it to the extreme, and anything was an excuse to drink.

My temper was getting worse, and I would regularly pick fights in bars or during sporting events. I was acting drunk even when I was sober. The alcohol gave me confidence and strength, and I would try to hold on to that feeling for as long as possible.

The edges were starting to fray. Drinking wasn't just fun anymore—it was medicine. And no matter what it was trying to treat, the symptoms kept getting worse. So I found something stronger.

# Take Two and Call No One

I blew out my knee playing soccer during my junior year at school. I wasn't on the *actual* soccer team—or even the club team. Just the kind of guy who showed up and went full throttle, whether it was intramural, frat league, or the schoolyard. Funny enough, I *was* offered admission to SUNY Oswego if I committed to wrestling. I shut that shit down faster than a teenager closing tabs when their mom walks in the room. I loved competing, but 5 a.m. runs in the rain and burpees on a rancid-smelling wrestling mat? No thank you.

It might have only been a fraternity league, but we approached it like our lives depended on it. Don't get me wrong—we didn't practice or do anything remotely disciplined. We didn't even take a break from drinking the night before game day. Quite the opposite. Half the time, guys were still drunk when we took the field. We took turns running to the sideline between plays to puke our guts out. Not exactly a Nike commercial. Gatorade, maybe—*For when you want to leave it all on the field.*

We played all kinds of sports: full-contact football (*sans* pads), deck hockey (*also sans* pads), softball, basketball—and I think we even had a dodgeball team. I can't remember.

The football games were insane—and really fucking dangerous. My fraternity wasn't very big or particularly tough. There were definitely no pro scouts watching from the sidelines. We did have a reputation for starting trouble, on and off the field. Some of us were legit athletes. Others... not so much. We didn't play for money or a trophy. We played for bragging rights. That might not sound like a big deal, but trust me—it *was*.

We played proper eleven-on-eleven, no equipment, no referees, no mercy. I played running back and outside linebacker—every play. The contact was brutal: headhunting, horse-collars, late hits, and whatever random acts of violence we could muster. We played rain or shine.

I remember one game against a frat where it looked like the average guy could bench press a Yugo. I'm not going to lie—it was *damn* scary. Like, piss-my-pants scary. That day it was snowing really heavy and probably five degrees—subzero with wind chill. We were in upstate NY, where having your nostrils freeze shut on a normal winter day wasn't even newsworthy.

There was ice under the snow, making the field feel like concrete. Being a running back on those days? Absolute torture. No traction, no cutting, no hope of beating anyone to the outside. Heck, I hardly had the ability to do those things with perfect weather conditions.

I wasn't exactly well-liked by the other fraternities for... various reasons. And the football field was the perfect setting for something *not entirely removed* from attempted murder. I could hear guys on the other team whispering about hitting me high, low, and every-where in between.

Midway through the game, I couldn't feel my hands, feet, or face. I felt like that Messy Marvin kid from A Christmas Story who gets his tongue stuck to the pole—except it wasn't just my tongue, it was my entire goddamn body. But hey—go team.

Our quarterback called yet another run. A handoff up the middle. As I hit the line of scrimmage, I got slammed by what felt like a double-decker bus... towing two more double-decker buses. It was their biggest lineman—a six-foot three-inch, 240-pound senior who practically lived at the gym. The kind of guy you *avoid* eye contact with at all costs.

I did avoid eye contact—because my face was now in the snow. He landed on top of me with every ounce of dead weight in his body. I laid there, unmoving, nose smashed into the ice, face down like a Looney Tunes character after falling ten stories—just waiting for the anvil to drop.

When I finally rolled over, I saw blood in the snow where my head had been. My nose was broken, and I couldn't even feel it. I tried to stand, but I couldn't put any weight on my left foot. My teammates helped me off the field—and eventually to the hospital.

Diagnosis: broken nose and a fractured foot.

I'd love to say that game was some kind of outlier. It wasn't. It's a miracle no one was killed in those games.

The only silver lining? That night, I ended up at that lineman's apartment for an after-game party. We laughed, did a bunch of coke, and let bygones be bygones.

The injury to my foot turned out to be a hairline fracture. I had to stay off it for a couple of weeks, but it healed quickly. My broken nose? I wore it like a badge of honor for as long as I could.

So yeah—that gives you a taste of the punishment we took on the field. Which makes it all the more ironic that the most devastating injury I ever had—at school or anywhere—happened on the soccer field that spring.

We didn't have an intramural soccer league the first two years I was at school. A few of us asked around, got some interest, and eventually rallied the fraternities to start one. Inaugural season, first game. None of us knew what to expect from the competition. I didn't care. I was just psyched to play.

I hadn't played organized soccer since I was maybe fifteen or sixteen at camp. I was pretty good—probably better at soccer than any other sport. I just didn't pursue it in high school. If I could go back and ditch wrestling for soccer, I would in a heartbeat.

Getting twisted into a Bavarian pretzel in front of a gym full of people wasn't exactly my dream scenario. Also, skin-tight polyester singlets and cauliflower ear weren't a flattering combo on me.

Anyway—game day. We get to the field and I realize I left my cleats at the house. I had turf shoes in the trunk and made the lazy decision not to go back.

I would regret it for the rest of my life.

Ten minutes into the game, I chased someone down the sideline and went in for a slide tackle. I'd done it a thousand times. But turf shoes don't grip grass like cleats. My foot caught in the dirt, and my knee twisted in a way that would've made Doogie Howser dry-heave into his scrubs.

I heard the pop. Hit the ground. The guy I tackled heard it too and called for help.

My knee was locked and already swelling to the size of a softball.

I was dating a girl named Tina at the time who was amazing at taking care of me. Smart, take-charge type. I remember she was really good at English and Literature so she would write my papers for me. She had one of those typewriters with the white-out feature. At the time, that was super high tech. She picked me up and took me straight to the hospital.

That alone was terrifying. This was bumfuck upstate NY. The town's main draw was probably the last Woolworths in America. I wouldn't have been surprised if the head surgeon also worked the register there part-time.

Everything moved fast. Tina handled the logistics. We met with the surgeon. They took x-rays and an MRI and confirmed that it was a torn ACL and torn meniscus. There was no way to avoid surgery, especially if I wanted to play sports again. So I put on my big boy pants and had surgery the next day. The whole thing was just surreal.

You'd think my parents would've rushed to campus as soon as they heard the news.. Nope. If my kid so much as broke a gel tip I would have been there before her nail hit the floor. Instead, my girlfriend called my mom and assured her she'd take care of me, and that was that.

Honestly, I didn't care. Having my parents there would've probably been more painful than the injury.

After surgery, I was prescribed painkillers—for the first time. I had never felt pain like that before. It was pretty unbearable. I was restless and uncomfortable. I couldn't stay at my house because my room was on the second floor. Also my roommates were clueless and my house was a complete disaster area. It was a safety hazard without the injury. So I stayed at Tina's house. It couldn't have been easy for her. She definitely went above and beyond. I'm certainly not an ideal patient.

Back then, prescribing opioids wasn't as regulated. Doctors handed out pills like Jujubes at the movie theater. I was given three months' worth of hydrocodone—with refills. No conversation about side effects. No warning about the dangers of addiction. No check-in with my parents. I was twenty. There were so many red flags. What were they thinking?

Opioids would eventually become my drug of choice—right behind alcohol. I had enough pills to last the rest of the semester. And in my senior year? I broke my hand in a fight with the rugby team. More pills. Less pain.

Painkillers were a completely different ballgame for me. They were easy. There was no pregame, sloppy night out or after party. They worked quickly. One pill and a beer and it wasn't long before I felt anesthetized. They didn't make me sick, or full. I didn't smell like alcohol so no one would even notice. It was also easier to control the buzz. Take one every four to six hours. Just like the doctor prescribed. After the first few weeks, the pain subsided and I didn't need the painkillers anymore but as far as my friends and family were concerned, I was still in agony. It would be a very long time before I took another painkiller as prescribed.

The painkillers were the perfect temporary solution to a lifelong problem. They killed the pain—literally and figuratively. What started with a script and a busted knee quickly became something much harder to walk away from. I wasn't chasing relief anymore—I was chasing *numb*. And the thing about numbness is, once you get used to it, feeling anything at all starts to hurt.

Even though the pills worked better than anything else ever had, they couldn't cure what was underneath it all—this aching need to feel like I mattered. So I went back to one of the only places I ever felt like I belonged: the stage.

# Cue the Pig's Blood

From the time I was Prince Chulalongkorn in the fifth grade, I always had it in the back of my mind that I wanted to be an actor. I don't think it was about mastering the craft or a love for the arts. I think it was about chasing that feeling—of setting out to do something and actually following through. Of stepping out of my comfort zone and pushing through the discomfort. Of belonging to something that made me feel whole, accepted, appreciated. Normal.

The rehearsals, the memorizing, the inside jokes, the camaraderie—even the stress. It was all shared. I didn't have to do those things alone. There was a bond. Something sacred. I didn't have to talk about my feelings, because we were all climbing the same mountain. We needed it for different reasons, but we all got something out of it. For me, it filled a void I couldn't explain. But the warmth disappeared when the show was over. The security blanket I had wrapped so tightly around my emotions was pulled off, leaving me cold and exposed. Alone again. The self-doubt always returned.

Acting didn't erase the pain—it just masked it. Like alcohol and drugs eventually would. For six or seven hours a day, I didn't have to be Jason. I was someone else. Wearing a disguise. A protective skin. If only I could live in it always.

I could have pursued acting. But it wasn't my passion. I didn't care if I was the best actor on the stage. I wanted to be great, sure. And I had some natural ability—I could perform, especially under pressure. But fear was always louder. Fear of embarrassment. Fear of failure. Fear of being seen as a fraud. The more success I had, the more I doubted it. Every compliment, every bit of praise was dismissed. *They feel bad for me. They don't want to hurt my feelings.* I always found a way to sabotage it.

The more success I achieved—career, writing, humor, being a husband, a dad—the more I believed I didn't deserve any of it. That belief kept me small. Scared. I wanted to keep acting. But I was terrified.

At sleepaway camp, I auditioned for the camp production of *Bye Bye Birdie*. I landed the part of Hugo Peabody. Nailed the audition. A natural fit. It was my first time on stage since fifth grade. Friends had pushed me into it. I joked about being a prince once. Didn't think they'd call me on it. But even though things were going well, I didn't feel the same spark. The self-doubt crept in. Eventually, I quit. Made up some excuse about needing to focus or whatever. Truth was, the fear was too much.

Same pattern. Different mask. Drugs. Alcohol. They worked. Until they didn't.

College came next. Despite knowing my fraternity brothers would bust my balls, I signed up for acting classes. I actually enjoyed it. I was like Troy from *High School Musical*—minus the singing, the dancing, the happy ending, and, especially, the jawline.

The drama kids were the real deal. They wanted to act for a living. They were amazing. Serious. Dedicated. I felt like a tourist. Like they were waiting for me to pull a prank mid-monologue. But I wasn't there to screw around. I gave it my all—scene after scene, improv after improv.

I developed a crush on one of the girls in class. Her name was Jolie. She was gorgeous. Like Meryl Streep meets Goldie Hawn—ridiculously talented but still felt like someone who'd split a grilled cheese with you. She was probably the only one who really noticed me. We got paired up for a few scenes, and I was under her spell. During one improv, she accidentally let out the tiniest, cutest little fart. Like a baby mouse. I know that sounds weird, but it sealed it for me—not a fetish thing, just... human. Real. She giggled, smiled, and I melted.

I liked her so much, I wrote a poem and left it anonymously on her windshield. Never told her it was me. Hoped she'd figure it out and confess her undying love. Turns out she was dating another guy in class—Cal. What a stupid name. Tall, decent-looking, and a total tool. Arrogant. Disrespectful. I fantasized about punching him in the stomach and her falling into my arms. Never happened.

Toward the middle of the semester, the professor announced the end-of-year production: *A Streetcar Named Desire*. No way in hell I was trying out for that. I wasn't about to brag about my role in *The King and I* as my ticket to center stage. I stayed quiet.

But then—the unexpected. The professor, who I thought barely knew I existed, told me he wanted me to audition for the lead. Stanley Kowalski. Marlon Brando's role. I panicked. Then said yes.

Maybe it was a people-pleasing thing. Or maybe I just wanted to feel chosen. Maybe I thought, for a second, that I actually belonged.

The day of auditions, my imposter syndrome kicked in full blast. I felt like Carrie. That inner voice screaming, *They're all gonna laugh at you!*

But I showed up. Seven guys auditioned. Most of them regulars. Including—of course—the douchebag boyfriend. I was nervous as hell. But when it was my turn, I let it rip. I screamed "Stella!" like Brando reincarnated. People looked stunned. Even the professor looked stunned.

Callbacks came out that afternoon. Two names left: me and him.

Take that, you smug little shit.

The next day was the final audition. A head-to-head scene. The famous "casting my pearls before swine" scene between Stanley and Blanche. Heavy stuff. Not exactly Prince Chulalongkorn material.

I wore a white tank top like Brando's. Just for good luck. Just to sell it. I was paired with Jolie—my crush. Cal was paired with someone else. She wasn't nearly as good. He was furious.

His performance? Solid. Really good.

Mine? I don't even remember. I blacked out. Something else took over. When it ended, even Jolie looked at me like she didn't know who I was. The class applauded. The professor clapped. I felt like Rudy getting carried off the field.

I floated out of the building like I'd just left my body behind. It was magic. I walked home, cracked a beer, and smiled. I wasn't even nervous about the results—I knew I'd nailed it. I'd get the part. I'd get the girl.

The next day, I got to class early to check the final cast list. A crowd had already gathered. She was there. Waiting to fall into my arms. Cue the music. Roll credits.

I looked at the list. My name wasn't next to Stanley.

It was Cal.

I scanned the list again. Twice. Three times. Maybe they forgot. Maybe it was a typo. Maybe I hallucinated the applause.

Nope. There it was—my name. Bottom of the page: "Poker buddy: Jason Mayo." One of Stanley's forgettable meathead friends with maybe five words of dialogue and the emotional range of an extra in a tampon commercial.

I felt my whole body collapse inward.

*Of course. Of fucking course.* I should've known. I'm not Brando. I'm not even Danny Zuko in a community theater production of *Grease*. I'm the guy they keep around for comic relief until the real actors take the stage.

The applause? Pity. The professor? Just being nice. Jolie? Probably laughed the second I walked out.

The voices were back. *You're not good enough. You're a joke. They saw through it. You've been exposed.*

And I smiled. Said, *I didn't want the part anyway.* Classic me—walk into the ring, get knocked the fuck out, and say I slipped on the mat.

The teacher pulled me aside. Said I was amazing. Said I had a shot next time. I nodded, thanked him. But I was already disappearing.

I never spoke to Jolie again. Sat in the back, half-stoned, watching rehearsals just to pass the class.

It was like I never existed.

*Cue the pig's blood.*

# Super Senior, Super Fucked

Normally, your last semester of college is when you cruise through electives, like The History of Napkin Folding, The Psychology of Petting Zoos, and Advanced Squirrel Spotting. You coast to the finish line, margarita in one hand, diploma in the other.

But that's not how mine went.

Nothing in college ever worked out quite the way I planned. Not that I didn't make plans—some of them were even halfway decent—but most of my "best laid" ones involved booze, drugs, and just enough self-sabotage to derail any forward momentum. So instead of walking across a stage with a cap and gown, I limped into my fifth year—aka my "super senior" year. Which is hilarious, because there was absolutely nothing super about it.

I was embarrassed. Ashamed. I felt like a failure for not graduating on time like a normal, semi-functioning human being. The consequences weren't just emotional—my mom had to take on more student loans she couldn't afford, I had to take more classes (which I was garbage at), and worst of all, I wouldn't get to walk at graduation. No big ceremony. No teary hugs. Just a diploma mailed to me with a final invoice. On the outside, you'd never know how much that wrecked me. But it did.

That said, there were a few upsides. I had six more months of fully sanctioned, all-expenses-paid debauchery. My best friend was also doing the super senior thing, and he was ready for one last lap. I'd just broken up with another hostage—I mean, girlfriend—so I was free again, staring down another semester of institutionalized adulthood avoidance.

At the time, I had a job delivering food for a local deli owned by this older guy named Ralph. It was a new spot, and I think I might've been his first and only employee. Ralph was a nice guy—definitely not a genius—but he treated me well. And ironically, I was more responsible with that job than I ever was with classes. I mean, class didn't pay for booze and drugs, right?

I delivered food with his beat-up white van that looked like the kind of vehicle they warn you about in after-school specials. The radio was stuck on a single AM station—Rush Limbaugh, day in and day out. His voice was like nails on a chalkboard dipped in pork fat and patriotic bullshit. The only silver lining was that it gave me just enough talking points to deliberate with Ralph about politics, which I milked for whatever it was worth.

Of course, I still took advantage of him. On nights I closed up, I'd make sandwiches for me and my roommate, swipe a few pints of Ben & Jerry's, and grab as many bags of chips as I could carry. It felt more like a perk than a misdemeanor. Ralph never said anything. Maybe he knew. Maybe he didn't want to.

That whole semester was a blur. I lived in a constant brownout. The only time I wasn't brownout drunk was when I was in a full blackout, and the only time I wasn't blacked out was when I was passed out—so, technically, still unconscious. I only know this because years later, when I was trying to make amends to, well, *everyone*, I had a really hard time distinguishing memory from myth.

I vaguely remembered having an issue with a fraternity brother over my ex-girlfriend. I'd broken up with her, but I heard rumors he was hooking up with her. I took exception to that—despite it being none of my business. I assumed there was some kind of bro code, but I guess that's more of a suggestion than a rule.

Later on, I confirmed the story with my best friend, who'd witnessed it. Apparently, I got blackout drunk, went to the guy's apartment, banged on the door screaming for him to come out. When nobody answered, I broke in and ransacked the place looking for him. Turns out he wasn't even there. (Thank God.) He never spoke to me again after that. Can't say I blame him. Others in the frat kept their distance, too. I was becoming a liability.

There was another night—one I barely remember—where I went to the bar with some friends, said I had to pee, and instead of coming back refreshed, I apparently ripped the toilet out of the floor and flooded the entire bathroom. Not even sure why. Maybe I was angry. Maybe I was channeling my inner Hulk. Either way, everyone had to pee in the street after that. You're welcome.

Then there was the time I pissed off my roommate—pretty much the only person left who still had my back. One night, I supposedly lined up every piece of glassware, every ceramic mug in our apartment (which was conveniently located *above a bar*) and used them as hockey pucks. I slapped shot after shot into the kitchen wall with my hockey stick like I was Mark Messier in the skills competition. He came home to a war zone of shattered glass and me passed out on the couch like it was just another Tuesday. I would've killed me if I were him.

I'd love to say all of this was because of the drinking and drugs. That if I'd just been sober, none of this would've happened. But apparently, I had chaos coded into me.

Because the worst thing that happened that semester? I was stone-cold sober.

I'd been sick for a week. Couldn't drink, couldn't smoke, couldn't even get out of bed. It was right after my latest breakup, and I was extra irritable from the withdrawal cocktail of boredom and a backlog of shit I hadn't even begun to unpack. My roommate persuaded me to go out for a bit—just to get some air.

We walked downtown to one of the quieter bars. One of our fraternity brothers was working the door as a bouncer, so I stayed outside and shot the shit with him while my roommate went in. And it felt... good. Like actually good. I was clear-headed. Present. Remembering things in real time instead of having to CSI my way through memories the next day.

Then the rugby team stumbled out of the bar.

They'd just won a game and were drunk, rowdy, and ready to chest-bump the world. We knew some of them, but for whatever reason, the rugby guys never liked us. I guess frats and sanctioned violence didn't mix.

I was mid-convo with my friend when one of them shoulder-bumped me on the way out, laughing like it was nothing. I turned around, trying to let it go, trying to just breathe—but then he looked back at me.

"You got a problem?" he said.

"Actually, yeah," I replied. "I fucking do."

I looked at my buddy, who had the "here we go again" face locked and loaded.

The rugby guy started to approach. And that's when I remembered the only fighting advice I'd ever gotten: *If he's bigger than you, throw the first punch.*

So I did.

I nailed him square in the nose. He dropped instantly, bounced off the brick wall behind him. I jumped on top and kept swinging. He didn't even get a punch off. I don't know when I blacked out, but I must've—because the next thing I knew, four or five guys were pulling me off him. My hand looked like a horror show. Just... mangled. I looked at my roommate, who'd come running out.

"I think I need to go to the hospital," I said.

And just like that, for the second time in college, I found myself under the knife—this time to get a metal plate and screws put into my shattered hand.

About a week later, I saw the guy at a party. He had a black eye and a gash above his nose. He apologized. I told him it was all good. He walked away, and I remember thinking: *I really fucked that dude up —and somehow I still lost the fight.*

There was one silver lining, though.

Another three-month prescription for painkillers.

A metal plate and some screws seemed like a small price to pay... for a full stash to carry me through the rest of the semester.

I didn't know it yet, but just around the corner—somewhere between a blackout and a busted hand—I was about to meet the only good thing that would come out of that year.

# The Mohawk, the Mixer, and the Moment

After I broke my hand, I had about two and a half months left in my college career. What a way to finish—limping around like Terry Fox in a knee brace, my hand wrapped in enough gauze and ACE bandages to choke every sea turtle in the Pacific. I was floating through the days in a perpetual buzz, courtesy of Dr. Keepmehighenberg. My goals were simple: pass my remaining classes, avoid any new injuries, and ration my painkillers to last the rest of the semester.

Academically, I was circling the drain. I'd fallen behind in credits, and I still had some core classes to finish—*Chemistry* being one of them. It wasn't that I couldn't handle the material. If I actually applied myself, I could've coasted by. I mean, we were at *Oneonta*, not Berkeley. My issue wasn't intelligence—it was priorities. Getting up and going to class always felt so... pedestrian. I was great at doing the maximum minimum. Also great at sitting next to the smartest kid in the room come exam time.

One snowy morning during junior year, my housemate and I drove to campus in arctic-level cold. We trudged a quarter-mile through the snow to get to class, stood outside the building, looked at each other... and wordlessly turned around, drove home, and spent the day doing bong hits instead. Again—not dumb, just chronically bad at making good decisions.

Math and science had always been my kryptonite. I was more of an English and social studies guy—left brain, right brain, right? I was already blowing it in Chem. There was a lecture hall and a lab component, both mandatory. You could cheat on a test and scrape by, but you couldn't fake attendance. This was the '90s. No AI. No Zoom. If you weren't there in the flesh, you weren't there.

Despite the academic panic, my social life (if you can call it that) still took priority. I wasn't as active in the fraternity at that point, but I still went to mixers—free booze and, if I was single, a fresh menu of potential emotional hostages.

Halloween weekend rolled around, and we had a mixer lined up with Phi Sigma. I didn't know much about them—just that they weren't exactly known for being hot. But that never stopped us.

It was a costume party. Naturally, my roommate and I waited until the last minute to figure ours out. My brilliant idea? We'd shave our heads into mohawks and dress like King Diamond from Mercyful Fate—because obviously nothing says *fun and approachable* like Danish black metal face paint.

It made no sense. But that was the point. Doing weird shit for no reason was kind of my thing. My buddy didn't care, as long as we had weed. So we hit the local barber, asked for two mohawk specials, and sealed our fate. We could've worn pirate hats. Wigs. Literally anything else. Instead, we went full mental patient chic.

Here's the thing—I *loved* the mohawk. It fit the vibe: *I'm barely holding it together inside, so might as well let the outside match.* My roommate, on the other hand, looked like Beetlejuice after the head-shrinking scene. He was not amused.

My ex, Tina, who still lived in our building and somehow didn't hate me, agreed to do our makeup. She leaned into it—made me look like a deranged street mime. I wore a black T-shirt, camo pants, sunglasses, and what looked like the end of a caveman club strapped to my injured hand. One part Iroquois, one part death metal, one part certified jackass.

We pre-gamed at the apartment—there was no way we could walk into that party without liquid courage. Normally, we'd do a "lock-in" before mixers: keg, a few cases of MD 20/20 (aka Mad Dog—a "fortified" wine so questionable it's banned in three dimensions), and no one left until it was gone. Which always escalated into shirtless, sweaty, borderline *Fight Club* energy. Exactly the condition sorority girls dream of in a romantic partner.

Once the chaos reached critical mass, the sisters arrived and the party officially began. The usual house music playlist: C+C Music Factory, "Jump Around" by House of Pain, and "Brown Eyed Girl" by Van Morrison—for some reason, that song got the girls horny. It was like a magic elixir for your ears. I hated it. As a metal guy, it was like getting trapped in my own personal jukebox from hell.

More booze. More painkillers. More floating.

I wandered through the party, trying to make small talk—forgetting that I looked like a guy recently escaped from a Norwegian prison. As I headed up the stairs, I saw her.

Everything stopped.

She was tall—maybe five feet seven inches—long dark brown hair, dark eyes, perfect smile, glowing. She looked like Winnie Cooper from *The Wonder Years*, but way sexier. Amid all the madness, she stood out like a flare in a pitch black sky.

I didn't want to hook up with her. I wanted to talk to her. Something told me: *Don't blow this. She could be the one, dumbass.*

She was standing with her friends, and I had no plan. I just inserted myself into their conversation like a human red flag. Her friends looked at me like they were about to mace me and dial 9-1-1, but she didn't flinch. She just smiled.

"Aren't you in my chemistry class?" she asked.

I panicked. Had I ever been to chemistry class? I nodded. "Yeah, I think so."

She told me she remembered me from a day when the professor called me up for something. Apparently, I was wearing a shirt with Hebrew lettering that, when flipped upside down, said *Go Fuck Yourself.* That definitely tracked.

We talked the rest of the party. Nothing heavy. Just conversation. She was cool, funny, present. I couldn't believe she was standing there, choosing to talk to me. I'd been with a lot of girls at school, had a bit of a reputation, but she was next level. Like, different solar system.

She said, "I'm Ronni, by the way." I told her my name, but hers was already etched into me. The second she smiled, I knew I'd never forget it.

She stepped away with her friends to use the bathroom. I'm sure they were holding a quick intervention about whether or not I was going to roofie her. While she was gone, one of my younger fraternity brothers came up to me.

"Dude, I can't believe you're talking to her."

"Why?" I asked.

"That's the girl who was voted Greek Goddess this semester."

"Oh," I said, trying to look cool. "Yeah. I knew that."

When she came back, I tried to act normal. Just keep my brain from leaking out of my ears. We talked until the party started winding down, and I asked if I could walk her home. To my absolute shock, she said yes.

We walked all the way to her place, just talking. No pretense. No pickup lines. It felt... easy. At her door, she thanked me, then asked if I wanted a ride home.

She had a red Jeep Cherokee.

With a car phone.

Back then, that was basically a spaceship—Gordon Gekko stuff.

I remember thinking: *She's gorgeous. Sweet. Cool.*

*And she's rich?*

*This can't be real.*

She drove me back to my place. We kissed briefly, and I left.

That was it.

No shame. No drama. No wreckage.

Just connection.

And I was smitten.

I had no idea that the girl I met at a Halloween party—on a night that could've easily been another mess in a long line of trainwrecks—would go on to become the Winnie Cooper to my Kevin Arnold.

After four of the most *not so* Wonder(ful) Years of my life, it felt like the universe finally handed me something worth holding on to.

It was, quite literally, the first night of the rest of my life.

# From Smurfs to Superballs—It Was Always There

Before the vodka.

Before the blackouts, the quiet regrets, and the broken promises—

There were Smurfs. And hockey cards. And a growing pile of guitars I absolutely did not need, could barely play, and loved with all the intensity of a man trying to fill a void with six strings and a whammy bar.

Long before I ever touched a drop of alcohol, my brain was already chasing dopamine like it owed it money. I didn't know it then, but the signs were everywhere. The obsession. The compulsion. The inability to just enjoy something casually like a normal human being. If I liked it, I collected it. If I had one, I needed twenty. Whatever it was, I had to have it. And if it gave me even a whisper of escape or excitement? I was all in.

I didn't just have a few Smurfs. I had a civilization. Papa Smurf, Brainy, Jokey with the exploding present. I literally had a suitcase full of them.

Around ten or eleven, I took a sharp left into petty theft and started stealing chrome caps off car tires in the neighborhood. You know, those shiny little valve stem covers? I didn't want to sell them. I didn't even know what they were called. I just wanted to collect them. They clicked together. They were shiny. They felt like secret treasure. It wasn't about mischief or rebellion. It was about dopamine. Control. That momentary rush of having something no one else did.

Hockey cards were a full-blown lifestyle. I'd open a new pack like I was defusing a bomb. The smell of cardboard, the papery stick of gum that could crack a molar, and the hope—every single time—that I'd pull a Gretzky rookie. Or a Messier. Or even some backup goalie who might end up a Hall of Famer. It didn't matter. I needed the rush more than the card.

Same thing with Super Balls. I didn't even bounce them. I just hoarded them. Dozens stuffed in drawers, rolled under beds, tucked in coat pockets like neon rubber talismans. The sound they made when you whipped one against the wall and it ricocheted off every surface was weirdly satisfying—especially when it nailed my little brother in the nuts.

Then came comic books. I was around ten when it started, but I didn't stop until my mid-thirties. At one point, I had subscriptions to six or seven titles. X-Men, Cap, Spidey, Fantastic Four, Daredevil, anything Marvel. Miss a month? Panic. Lose a copy? Spiraling. Tell myself I was done? Not a chance. It was structure and escape at the same time.

The fidget spinner phase was supposed to help me stop biting my nails. One spinner. That's it. Just a tool. Then I got another. Then one that lit up. Then one with skulls on it. Before I knew it, I had a collection of about fifty. They weren't helping my nail-biting, but they were definitely helping my dopamine system stay on life support.

But nothing says "this brain is wired for more" quite like my guitar wall. I started playing when I was thirteen, and to this day, I can only reliably play three things: the riff from Dio's "Rainbow in the Dark," the opening of "Crazy Train," and "Rock You Like a Hurricane." That one I can play in its entirety. That's it. Three power chords and a dream. And yet I own thirteen guitars. They hang on the wall like trophies of a Rock & Roll Hall of Famer. One of them is a seven-string, which I bought without realizing I don't even know how to tune a seven-string. But it looked cool. So why not.

Then there were the CDs. And the cassettes. And the vinyl. I bought entire albums because of the cover art. Lined them up alphabetically. Reorganized them by mood. Then by decade. Books? Don't even get me started. Read a few. Bought a few hundred. Still have stacks of them, untouched, but somehow deeply meaningful just by existing in my space. Even now, I can't walk into a bookstore without buying some random coffee table book about the history of the tiny home or a book of short stories by indie authors that no one has even heard of.

So yeah. The signs were there. Long before the drinking. Long before the wreckage. My brain has always been like this—wired for more. More novelty. More escape. More curating, more chasing, more rituals to make me feel like I'm okay.

I didn't drink because I was broken. I drank because I was already primed to fixate. And alcohol was just the fastest shortcut to feeling lit up, calm, numb, connected—whatever the feeling of the day required.

It wasn't just addiction. It was the operating system I'd been running on since I was a kid.

The vodka just showed up late to the party.

The addiction was always there.

It just started in a Toys R Us.

# I Am the Scrunchy King

The rest of that semester didn't even feel like college.

I had found the answer to all of my demons in the form of the perfect woman. It's like I accidentally kicked over a lamp at a frat party and released a genie. Wish granted.

Suddenly everything seemed easier. Lighter. Less urgent. I was still drinking and doing drugs—but not with the same reckless abandon. I didn't want to fuck up the one subject in college that might actually stick: Ronni.

She was it. The only thing that made me want to try.

I was all in.

I was sweet. I was kind. I was writing poetry again. Writing lyrics. Playing guitar. I was still me—funny, hard-partying, academically subpar—but with one major difference: I wasn't shitfaced every second of the day.

That might sound like nothing. But for me, it was huge.

I didn't need alcohol and drugs to numb the pain. I had just... replaced it. Put something else in its place. That had been the pattern my whole life—but this time, I convinced myself it was different. Maybe I was just clinging to the last safety net I had before college ended and the bottom dropped out. Or maybe this was real. Soulmate-level shit. The kind they talk about in Meg Ryan movies.

Whatever it was, I knew one thing for sure: *time was not a luxury I had.*

I started skipping fraternity parties and mixers. Every free night, every free minute—I wanted to be with her. I thought about her constantly. That face and that cute little laugh that sounded like she had a secret she couldn't keep. Hell, I even started going to class. *Chemistry*, at least. I honestly think I would've failed that class if I hadn't met her.

We sat together in lecture hall. We weren't lab partners, but I'd find excuses to hang around. Make stupid jokes.

"Hey, is that a Bunsen burner in your pocket, or are you just happy to see me?"

I was like a kid with his first crush. That same euphoria I used to chase with booze and drugs—I was feeling it without a drop. Make no mistake, I was still high—just on something else.

It almost made me forget my addiction. Or at least downplay it.

Maybe I wasn't such a fuckup. Maybe I wasn't broken. Maybe she was the glue that could hold me together.

But love isn't magic—it's an IKEA couch. Follow the instructions. And if you're missing even one little piece, it's only a matter of time before the whole thing collapses.

And someone gets hurt.

I loved going to her house. It was a new scene, totally different from mine. Fresh air. Her roommates were the same ones who'd warned her about me that night at the Halloween party—Jody and Melissa. They were still skeptical—but I was determined to prove them wrong.

They were actually kind of hilarious. I became a fixture at the house, and they didn't seem to mind. But I wasn't dumb—I knew I wasn't just courting *Ronni*. I was courting them.

Courting her was easy. Holding doors. Buying dinner. Bringing flowers. Writing poetry. Textbook stuff. It felt natural. But I'd also spent my entire life being a master manipulator—not in a malicious way, but in that "everything's fine, nothing to see here" kind of way. I could reinvent myself in any room. Just like summer camp. Just like coming to college. Another first impression to nail. I always seemed like a catch at first—until I turned from a three-hundred-pound tuna into a moldy tire covered in seaweed and a flip-flop.

I still worked for Ralph at the deli, so I had access to an endless supply of sandwiches, snacks, and Ben & Jerry's. My friends got screwed—everything went straight to Ronni and her roommates. I came bearing gifts. Jewels and riches in the form of Bugles and Phish Food ice cream.

My old housemate Moose had a side hustle selling scrunchies—those colorful, ruffled hair ties that practically lived on every girl's wrist in the '80s. They were basically currency back then. When he graduated, he left behind a garbage bag full of them. For months, they just sat there collecting dust—until I started bringing them to Ronni's house. I'd drop off a new assortment each time. Nothing special, but Ronni and her roommates thought it was adorable. Just another distraction from who I really was under all the charm.

Moose and I lived in a big house off campus on Oak Street. It was technically the main fraternity house, but calling it a house feels generous—it was more like a poorly supervised biohazard experiment. Broken dishes and glasses everywhere. Days-old food left out like science fair projects. We'd make spaghetti and meat sauce, leave it out, and pick at it throughout the week like raccoons in basketball shorts. I'm genuinely shocked we didn't end up with a tapeworm the size of a firehose.

We had another housemate we nicknamed "Mork"—because he acted like he was from another planet and drove a tiny lime green Volkswagen we called the Mork Mobile. He was hilarious without meaning to be, like watching a gorilla trying to use a Shake Weight. Always doing something bizarre.

One time, at the end of the semester, I left early for summer break and trusted Moose and Mork to lock up. Which they did. But not before hosting a lobster dinner and leaving the trash—full of shells, butter-soaked napkins, and claw bits—inside the house. In July. For two months. No A/C. I came back first—with my girlfriend at the time—and realized I forgot my key. So naturally, I punched through the front door window (not the first time), walked in, and immediately projectile vomited in the living room. The smell? Like Satan hosted a clam bake in a port-a-potty at Lollapalooza—mid-heatwave, day three, no toilet paper. I found the garbage can open on the kitchen floor with a thousand maggots throwing a rave on what used to be dinner. I turned right around and left without calling Moose or Mork. Let 'em walk into that horror show like I did.

Oh, and just to round out the hellscape—we lived fifteen feet from an elementary school. Which wouldn't have been a big deal, except Mork once decided to bring up a couple ounces of cocaine to sell to our frat brothers—like he was setting up a fucking bake sale. Nothing like pushing product in view of the monkey bars. When we realized how bad that could end, we made the obviously responsible choice: to do it ourselves. You know, for safety. That semester went from Budweiser and bongs to coke lines and NyQuil chasers. We should've died. Or at least been arrested. But somehow, we just... kept going.

Now, I wasn't a bad guy. I need you to know that.

I always wanted to do the right thing. I meant well. I was kind, sensitive, empathetic.

But I was sick. Very sick.

When I got sober, I heard someone in a meeting say:

"We're not bad people getting good. We're sick people getting well."

That hit me like a freight train. It's sad, really. Not every alcoholic is some guy passed out on a park bench. Not everyone with mental illness belongs in a padded room. I could write a whole book on stigma—and maybe someday I will—but this isn't that story.

Still, I like to think the guy Ronni met in the beginning—the guy who made her laugh and brought ice cream and scrunchies to her friends—that *was* the real me. But Dr. Jekyll always gives way to Mr. Hyde eventually. It's not his fault. It just *is*.

Her friends liked to party. Not like me. Not like my friends. But they didn't mind when I busted out a joint or made a bong out of an apple. Sometimes they'd even come to my place, smoke a little, watch a movie. I was a bad influence—but at first, it felt harmless.

Ronni, though? She barely drank. Had never smoked a cigarette. Had never tried drugs. She actually *was* a real-life Winnie Cooper.

*I changed that right away.*

I had to—because if she tried it, then it couldn't be that bad.

See? Everyone does it. It's fine.

The pills?

*No one* ever knew about those. Especially not Ronni. That cat stayed in the bag for a long, long time.

As the semester came to a close, I started getting nervous. Paranoid. Sad.

She'd be going back to school in the fall. I'd be home. She'd be doing her own thing. Other guys would hit on her—maybe even my old fraternity brothers. The thought made my skin crawl.

I kept it all to myself. I didn't want to look needy. Not yet.

But the screws on that IKEA couch were already starting to loosen. And she hadn't even sat down yet.

Still, for a little while, I had them all fooled. I was the funny guy. The poetry guy. The guy with ice cream and Bugles and an unlimited supply of vintage hair ties.

I was the Scrunchie King.

And for a moment, that crown almost fit.

# Foreskin, Fire, and Friendship

When I was old enough, my mom decided to send me and my brother to sleepaway camp. I had already been a veteran of the day camp circuit and would have been perfectly happy continuing on that track, but either my mother thought that the time away would be good for me—a change of scenery maybe—or she just needed a fucking well-deserved break from the day in and day out of raising two angry, resentful little shits. Boys in general are hard enough for a two-parent household, but a single mom? Forget it. If I had been her, I would have shipped us off to boarding school somewhere in the North Pacific.

I was twelve at the time. Not yet a man in the traditional Judaica sense, but with the weight of the world on my shoulders and my lived experience, I probably had the mental age of a forty-eight-year-old ironworker with the emotional capacity of a toddler.

The camp was called Lakewood. It was out in the boondocks of Pennsylvania about four hours away from home. Like the day camp we went to, it was also a Jewish Federation camp. Again, it just feels wrong to put Jewish and camp in the same sentence. I can't stress that enough. There were actually two camps in one. There was a huge lake, and on one side of the lake was Ridgewood. This was for ages probably as young as six, all the way up to twelve. On the other side of the lake was Lakewood. This was the older kid camp. That's where all of the action happened. Kind of like comparing *Meatballs* to *Fast Times at Ridgemont High* with a smidge of *Porky's*. Both were really fun but definitely with different vibes.

They were both extremely low budget, which is a kind way of saying it was a complete shithole. The equipment was old, the cabins looked like sheds held together by rusty nails, the food was probably one step up from what was served in an internment camp, the fields were half dirt / half burnt-out grass, and the bathrooms smelled like mold and dirty jockstraps—like someone had Febreezed a crime scene. The counselors were mostly from Europe on an exchange program. They would spend the summer at the camp, all expenses paid, and then after the summer they would tour the U.S. for a while and head home. They seemed beyond excited to be there and were way happier and more fun than the American counselors.

There were two things about the European staff that separated them from anything I had ever experienced before—the guys in particular. They all had extreme body odor. They smelled like onions. And they all had weird-looking junk and they weren't shy about it. As a nice Jewish kid from Long Island, I had never been exposed to foreskin before. This was absolutely frightening. They all looked like they had burnt bratwurst hanging from their midsection. The bathrooms were wide open, so when you showered, everyone could see you. It was embarrassing and humiliating. I always walked around with a towel until the last second and showered facing the wall like I was in prison or something. That would never fly today. Everyone would have their own private stall with a double steel door and a lock as big as the vault in Fort Knox.

There was also something called a Bradley. It was a big round fountain, kind of like a wishing well but with purpose. I'm not sure what the purpose was, but I think it might have been to rinse off your bathing suit or something. Instead, kids pissed in it, and if you were unlucky enough, you got thrown in. Usually naked. That whole bathroom scene was straight up nightmare fuel.

There was also something called a rat-tail. This is when you would soak your towel so it was really heavy, wind it up tightly, and whip someone right in the ass. Like, really snap it so it made a sound and left a mark. It was only the strongest survive. Darwin-type shit.

We did some fun stuff in the bathroom, too. We played a game called doodie baseball. That was a highlight, and I actually got pretty good at it. When you were making a doodie in one stall and your friend was in the next stall, you kept score. No splash? Out. Splash on the left cheek? Single. Right cheek? Double. Both cheeks? Triple. Right up the bunghole? Home run. If you peed, it was a rain delay. Classic.

To this day, I wish I could bust into a game of doodie baseball at work or in a public restroom, but I'd probably go to jail. We also had something called skydiving. This is when you climbed up to the top of the stall, one foot balanced on either side of the stall walls, legs spread wide, and you would try to shit into the toilet bowl. Disgusting, but also a feat of athletic superiority. I feel bad for the poor bastard who had to clean that bathroom—probably some unlucky European counselor questioning every life decision he'd ever made.

The cabins were borderline condemnable. They were old wooden sheds with two bunk beds, one on either side, and usually a cot in the middle. There was graffiti from all the years past on the walls, and the mattresses were thinner than—and more uncomfortable than—a piece of cardboard. It was an absolute hotbox during the day and an icebox at night. Not only were there five kids crammed in there, there were mice that were squatting as well. Or maybe they lived there and we were squatting. You'd hear them scurrying at night, just hoping one wouldn't wind up in your mouth while you were sleeping. They set traps, so we'd sometimes hear one struggling to escape, gnawing at its own leg to break free. If it was still alive, a counselor would come to the bunk, bring the trap outside, and crush the mouse with a rock.

Not sure if my mom even looked at a brochure before she picked this camp, but you get what you get and you don't get upset, I suppose.

With all that being said—it was fucking amazeballs. Day camp was fun and all, but the feeling of being away from home and on my own, so to speak, was something I had never experienced before. Independence. It didn't matter that the camp wasn't fancy, that the counselors had weird-looking penises, or that I could've caught a disease from a rabid mouse bite in the dead of night. I didn't know any better and we were all in it together—so it was ours.

At first, I was nervous. Even though I was pretty Teflon on the outside, I was still fragile and broken on the inside, and I had no idea if anyone would accept me or like me. I was totally wrong. The second I stepped off the bus, they did roll call and put us into groups —B1, B2, B3, B4, and B5. That summer, I was in B2. There was a kid named Ray. I met him first.

He was my age but looked like he was in his early thirties. Dark hair, fish lips, and built like a junior Olympic wrestler. He looked like he could have played Matt Dillon's third cousin in a sequel to The Outsiders. He was loud, confident, and cool. Cracking jokes like he was Jackie Mason's grandkid. He was hilarious. Everyone gravitated toward him like he was Jesus preaching to his disciples. We hit it off right away. Even though he was holding court like he owned the place, I'm sure he was just as scared as I was—he just handled it differently.

That summer we became fast friends. Inseparable. People always thought we were brothers. We liked the same music—AC/DC, Queen, and The Police. He brought a boom box and blasted music constantly, singing along and mimicking Brian Johnson, Freddie Mercury, and Sting. He was terrible, but it cracked everyone up.

Ray played hockey. Not just roller hockey in the street—ice hockey, in an actual league. That blew my mind. Eventually, he'd play roller with my friends back home and skate literal circles around us. Ray was good at everything—softball, soccer, hockey, basketball, dodgeball, tetherball, football. You name it. He was always the first pick.

We both kept coming back every summer. Sometimes we'd visit during the year. He lived way out on the other side of the island, so it always felt like a road trip to get there, but we always picked up right where we left off.

As we got older, the friendship only got stronger. I had my best friends at home, but Ray and my other camp friends were a different kind of bond. Camp friendships are like reality-show relationships on speed. Two months felt like two years. We spent day and night together. Eventually, we both started paying attention to the girls. Ray always had a girlfriend—always one of the popular, good-looking ones.

We started working out together. Ray turned into a teenage Lou Ferrigno. I was more McCauley Culkin. But together, we were unstoppable: camp's answer to a buddy cop film that never got greenlit. I was the camp clown; between us, every interaction was like a full-on comedy show. Even the counselors loved hanging out with us. Ray was more daring than me. He got in trouble often. He wasn't afraid to talk back to counselors or even the camp director. It made me nervous, but people loved him for it.

At sixteen, we became LITs—Leaders in Training. Supervised? Not really. The European counselors weren't exactly role models. One summer, Ray had the idea to pierce our ears. It was cool to have one earring—in the left ear. Not the right. Right meant you were gay. Don't ask me why.

Ray brought two fake diamond studs to camp. No piercing gun. No plan. He stole ice from the kitchen to numb his ear and just pushed the stud through with his fingers. Blood everywhere. He laughed like a maniac. Then it was my turn. I didn't even want the earring, but Ray was the arbiter of cool. I hesitated. He coached me like Mickey yelling at Rocky. I forced it through. I thought I was going to faint. Somehow, neither of us got infected. We were the first guys in camp to rock earrings. We were proud. It was our blood pact.

That last summer before college, Ray was heading to Oswego State and I to Oneonta. He wasn't book smart—people thought he was a lovable idiot—but I always thought he was smarter than he let on. That summer was bittersweet. I had a girlfriend from home I really cared about, but I bailed on her for camp. Like most of my relationships, I was already pulling away. Self-protection disguised as boredom. Another brick in the wall around my heart.

By then, Ray and I were on our own paths of substance abuse. I was drinking alone more. He was drinking and smoking weed regularly. We were seventeen, CAs—counselors' assistants—with more freedom. We couldn't really drink during the day, but nights were fair game. One kid in the oldest bunk brought weed. Ray found it and "confiscated" it, meaning we now had weed to go with our beer.

One day off, Ray, me, and our buddy Matt—our third musketeer— hiked to Blueberry Hill with a cooler of Budweisers and a few joints. Matt was like the Ferris Bueller of camp. Good-looking, witty, athletic. He was also the responsible one. The one who drank less to keep us from dying.

We got obliterated. No food. No water. We lost track of time and tried to hike back. Took a wrong turn and came out by the lake. Kids and staff were all there. Beers floating out of the cooler. We looked like drunk Sherpas. Somehow we didn't get kicked out. But after that, we weren't golden boys anymore. We were derelicts. Matt kept his rep clean. He went on to become a pediatric oncologist. The guy kept photos of sick kids in his wallet. That's who he was.

About a week later, Ray mouthed off to a counselor. That night, he slashed the guy's tires in a drunken stupor. The next morning, the camp director woke him up and kicked him out. Just like that—he was gone. My best friend. My reason for being there. I was devastated.

A few days later, we were all in the dining hall at dinner. Saul, the camp director, was making announcements. I was talking to one of the kids—not trying to be disrespectful, just distracted—and he called me out. Loud. In front of everyone.

It was like getting shushed by your rabbi in temple—but this wasn't just about me talking.

I was already raw. I was grieving Ray being gone, trying to pretend everything was fine, when nothing was.

My pride kicked in. My fuse lit.

I stormed out, packed my shit, and made up my mind to leave.

That's when Helen, Saul's wife—someone I adored, someone who always treated me like family—came running after me. She wasn't yelling. She wasn't scolding. She was crying. Begging me not to go. Telling me I was loved, that I belonged there, that this didn't have to be how it ended.

And I stood there, barely holding myself together, knowing she was right, knowing I didn't want to leave, but already halfway gone in my mind. She tried to hug me, I said something weak and final, and drove off with the whole camp watching me go.

I've made a lot of bad decisions in my life. But that one—that moment—still lives in me like a stone in my stomach. I left the one place where I had truly felt seen, felt safe. And I left it angry. Alone. Ashamed. Like I always did.

That wasn't the last time I'd bulldoze my own comfort for no good reason. It was just the beginning. My anger was always simmering. My fuse kept getting shorter. I didn't know how to feel anything deeper than surface level.

So I ran. Even when it was the last thing I wanted to do.

# Mullets, Mice, and Missed Opportunities

In the four-and-a-half years it took me to graduate from college, I never really thought seriously about what I wanted to do for a living.

I didn't have a plan, a passion, or even a half-baked idea.

A few of my cousins on my dad's side were public defenders for Legal Aid. I looked up to them—anything they did seemed noble and heroic.

They told me if I went to law school and passed the bar, they'd definitely hook me up with a job.

Not sure why they thought I was lawyer material.

Maybe I argued with them in a blackout and left a lasting impression.

Who knows.

When I was registering for freshman classes, I thought maybe pre-law was the move.

I imagined myself breezing through law school and somehow ending up trying cases with Alan Dershowitz.

Didn't happen.

Instead, after one semester of pre-law and a 1.67 GPA, I switched to Speech Communications because it sounded easier than Business Economics.

I didn't consult an advisor.

I didn't weigh my options.

I just did it.

I did it like almost every decision I made in college—impulsively and half-conscious.

The truth is, even back then, I had the acting bug. It ended badly with college theater, but somewhere in my head, I kept the dream alive.

Someday, I'd give it a real shot.

Someday, I'd get headshots taken at the mall, go on a couple auditions, and next thing you know, I'd be co-starring with Ralph Macchio in *Karate Kid 4: Wax Harder*.

That was the pattern.

I always had big plans—rockstar, novelist, actor.

But the second anything got hard or scary, I bailed.

It wasn't the dream I wanted.

It was the idea that people would *think* I was good enough to chase it.

It was always easier to build the image than to face the fear that maybe—deep down—I wasn't good enough at all.

As graduation approached, panic started setting in.

I needed something—anything—before I ended up back home slinging roast beef sandwiches at Arby's for old high school classmates on their lunch breaks.

Nothing says "bright future" like Horsey Sauce under your fingernails.

Through a connection of my mom's—a friend from Parents Without Partners—I got introduced to her ex-husband, Gary.

He owned a small production company in New York City called Metro Video.

They did real commercials for TV—not just local public access stuff.

It felt like fate.

I figured it was perfect. Work behind the scenes, meet the right people, and get discovered.

Voilà!—the next Corey.

Gary told me to come into the city to meet him and check out the studio. I couldn't wait.

It was about 100 degrees the day I took the train into Manhattan.

I was wearing khakis and a silk, floral button-down shirt.

And I had the mullet—business up front, party in the back.

By the time I found the office, I looked like I'd gone through a car wash.

The silk shirt was soaked and sticking to me like wet newspaper.

Of course, no undershirt. Why plan ahead?

I begged the receptionist to use the bathroom, squeezed into a tiny, airless cubicle of a restroom, and tried to dry myself off with toilet paper.

Instead, I just managed to glue little bits of wet tissue to my chest hair and the back of my neck.

Good start.

Gary finally came out to greet me.

He wasn't what I expected—about five feet eight inches, balding with a sad little ponytail, and a voice that sounded like Casey Kasem introducing the week's number one song in America.

He talked at me for an hour—mostly about his ex-wife, flying planes, his voiceover gigs. Never once asked about me. Which, honestly, was fine because I didn't know what the hell I would've said.

At the end of the meeting, he offered me a job—after graduation—as the receptionist.

I said yes right away.

I floated out of there like I had just landed a major studio deal.

This was it.

I wasn't going to be stuck at Arby's.

I was going to work in *the city*.

Big time.

After graduation, I called Gary and asked when he wanted me to start.

I was living at home to save money, so commuting into the city didn't seem like a big deal.

Train fare, lunch, and that was it.

I had never even asked what the salary was.

I figured it had to be better than minimum wage.

It wasn't.

Thirteen thousand dollars a year.

After taxes, I could barely afford a train ticket, a bodega sandwich, and maybe a pouch of Big League Chew if I found change in the couch cushions.

Still, I was excited.

And terrified.

Because underneath it all, everything felt shaky.

Ronni still had another year of school.

We talked almost every night.

I missed her constantly.

I worried nonstop that long distance would kill us. That she'd meet someone else. That I was already being left behind.

I wrote her letters.

I sent her little gifts from street vendors—stuff she probably hated, but I meant well.

I never told her how little I was making.

I didn't want her to know how small and scared I felt.

I lied by omission.

Like I did with almost everything real.

When I wasn't missing her, I was drinking.

Mostly at home.

Sometimes with coworkers.

We'd sneak beer back to the office after hours and get buzzed watching the latest *Seinfeld*. Mostly though, it was solo—sitting in my bedroom at home, feeling like a failure at the ripe old age of twenty-one.

My first week on the job was easy.

Answering phones.

Smiling.

Being invisible.

The outgoing receptionist trained me.

She was beautiful—blond, funny.

Turned out, she was a former child star from *Hazel*, a '60s sitcom.

She even called Jack Klugman—Oscar Madison from *The Odd Couple*—so I could say hi. I almost fainted.

When he answered, his voice was raspy and broken.

I didn't know he had survived throat cancer.

At first, I thought I was on an episode of *Punk'd*.

But it *was* him.

He was kind.

Later, he even sent me an autographed photo.

No launch into Hollywood stardom, but still—a cool moment.

After a few months, Gary told me he was promoting me to "coordinator."

I thought that meant I was moving up.

Bigger responsibilities.

More respect.

Not exactly.

It meant getting to the office early to open the building, running errands and handling problems nobody else wanted to touch.

The problems were *legendary.*

**First,** there was the doo-doo left by homeless guy who used our front stoop as his personal toilet every night.

Every morning, there'd be a fresh pile waiting for me.

Dry-heaving and cursing my life, I had to hose it off before clients showed up.

**Second,** the mice.

They lived—and died—in the drop ceiling.

When the smell got bad enough, someone had to go up, pop the ceiling tiles, and extricate the corpses.

Guess who got that job?

I climbed shaky ladders with a broomstick, poking around, praying a dead mouse wouldn't fall into my face.

Dry-heaving became a regular part of my morning routine.

**Third,** heavy lifting.

When Gary needed thirty heavy boxes moved into storage, I happened to be wearing—you guessed it—my silk floral shirt again.

I asked if we could wait until tomorrow so I could change. Gary said no but offered me a gym T-shirt he had just sweat through that morning. It smelled like armpits and hot dog water. I wore it anyway.

Because what the hell else could I do?

One afternoon, Gary asked if I could cover for the assistant editor.

The regular guy was out, and Gary needed someone to help with a project.

It was a great opportunity.

I knew how to do most of the basics.

I had been watching and learning.

I could have stepped in, no problem.

But instead of just saying yes, I hesitated.

I told him I needed to check if I had plans.

The truth was, I had been planning to talk to Ronni that night.

We hadn't spoken in a couple of days, and I didn't want to screw it up.

I missed her so much it hurt sometimes, and that call felt like the only thing tethering me to something real.

Gary looked at me—not mad, just disappointed and very clear. He said:

"If you're gonna make it in this business, you gotta say yes to opportunity. If you have plans, that's fine this time. But next time, this comes first."

I went downstairs, stared at the phone, thought about it.

*Work or love.*

The beginning of a choice I would have to make over and over again.

I told Gary I could do it.

He'd already found somebody else.

It crushed me.

Not just because I missed out on the editing gig.

Because, for the first time, I felt like someone had caught me being... ordinary.

Not hungry enough.

Not serious enough.

Not special.

I hated it.

I hated the idea that Gary thought I wasn't willing to go above and beyond.

That I was just another kid who didn't get it.

I didn't want to be that guy.

I wanted to be the one people could count on.

The one people bragged about.

The most valuable player.

Something shifted inside me that day.

I didn't say no anymore.

Not to work.

Not to opportunity.

Not to anything that might make me look good, get ahead, or prove I was worth betting on.

From then on, every time someone offered a chance—no matter how small—I jumped at it.

Because I never again wanted anyone to see me as ordinary.

And slowly, without even realizing it, work became my new addiction.

It filled the same hole.

The same rush.

The same desperation to feel needed. Important. Enough.

I didn't have the words for it then.

I just knew that next time, I wouldn't hesitate.

Next time, I'd say yes. But the next time never came.

After almost a year of humiliation and dry-heaving, I decided I deserved a raise.

I asked Gary for $25,000.

He said he'd think about it.

At the end of the week, he called me in and—smiling like he was giving me the keys to a new Mercedes—offered me $15,000.

Fifteen thousand dollars.

Cue sad trombone.

I thanked him like an idiot.

That night, I stayed late, printed out a hundred résumés using his printer, his paper, and his postage machine.

I mailed every single one out to production houses across the tri-state area.

Of course, being me, I didn't load enough paper into the printer.

The next morning, my résumés started flying out like ticker tape on the New York Stock Exchange. Gary found them and called me into his office, holding the stack like a disappointed dad.

"Nice résumé, Jason," he said. "Trying to tell me something?"

Insert tail between legs.

A week later, I got an offer.

Another production house.

Entry-level.

$20,000 a year.

I took it faster than the homeless guy could pull his pants up after his late-night visit.

I was out.

Still pretending.

Still lost.

But moving forward.

I hated that job.

I hated cleaning shit off the stoop, picking up dead mice, and smelling like a gym sock for $13,000 a year.

But looking back, I can see it for what it was: my first real shot.

Gary gave me that.

He didn't have to.

I was a clueless kid with no experience and no idea what I was doing, and he gave me a place to start.

At the time, all I could feel was resentment.

I didn't know how to be grateful yet.

Years later, when I heard that Gary had died, it hit me harder than I expected.

Not because we stayed close—we didn't—but because he's part of my story.

The first step.

The first push out of the nest.

The first place where I started becoming whoever it is I'm still trying to be.

# Stay Groovy

It's hard to describe my Uncle Larry. He wasn't just my Uncle Larry—he was *everybody's* Uncle Larry. Dude was a full-blown legend.

He was my mom's younger brother, but they were polar opposites. My mom, even with her great sense of humor, was the more serious, responsible one. Larry? Larry was Peter Pan in flip flops. He refused to grow up.

Whenever he was around, it felt like someone had snuck a keg into a library. Joking, pranking, laughing—half the time he couldn't even keep himself together. He was the guy you didn't want to sit next to during a funeral eulogy. Not because he'd cry—because he'd laugh. I'm talking all-out, face-turns-beet-red, tears-streaming, body-shaking, can't-breathe *hysteria*. It was a scene.

I honestly don't know how he survived growing up with my grandparents. They were strict, religious, and proper—the type who could weaponize disappointment like a sniper rifle. I wonder how many slippers he took to the side of the head from my grandma over the years.

Larry was born hard of hearing. My mom was, too, but she adapted —speech therapy, lip reading, hearing aids. You'd never know if you met her. Larry... not so much. Even with his hearing aids cranked to "these go to eleven," he was basically deaf. Didn't slow him down for a second.

He was literally the poster boy for the League for the Hard of Hearing when he was a kid—Howdy Doody grin and all. He loved telling people that.

He looked like a cartoon character designed by a stoned Disney animator: five feet five inches, 130 pounds soaking wet, blue jeans, two-tone leather Justin cowboy boots with detailed stitching, a denim button-down shirt with its sleeves hacked off at the shoulders (and tucked aggressively into said jeans), a multicolored patterned fabric belt, and a massive Native American belt buckle from New Mexico. Turquoise bracelets were stacked up both arms like he was trying to communicate with satellites, and there was always a different colored bandana tied around his head, like a semiretired roadie for Crosby, Stills, and Nash.

For my birthday the year I lived with him, he bought me a pair of black Justin boots. They must have cost $400. Larry always asked if I liked his boots, and of course, I always said yes just to appease him. In reality, I hated them. I thought they were hideous. So naturally, he thought I would *love* them.

First of all, they were a size too small. They had pointy toes so sharp I felt like a little Chinese girl after foot-binding. And they had these high heels that made walking feel like trying to cross a balance beam in a hurricane.

But because I lived with him, I had to wear them. No way out.

So I stashed a pair of sneakers in my backpack every morning and snuck them to work. I would round the corner toward the subway, wait until I was out of sight, and swap them out as fast as I could. I must have looked like a fugitive cowboy on the lam, ditching his boots before the sheriff caught up.

When he was younger, he had a massive red Jewfro, but by his early twenties, the top had surrendered, leaving him with the classic Gallagher horseshoe. He held onto a tiny, withered ponytail well into his sixties—like it was part of a hostage negotiation. Pretty sure it whispered at night, "Please... just let me go."

And the mustache. Larry always rocked the mustache. Never backed down. From Tom Selleck to the Village People, he *owned* it.

His vocabulary never made it out of the seventies, either. "Right on." "Groovy." Every time he said goodbye, he'd flash a peace sign and say, "Stay groovy." Nobody talks like that anymore. Shame.

In my teens, Larry ran a house-share in Fire Island, back when Fire Island was still half-feral and barely on the map. It was his happy place—bare feet, fruity cocktails, sunburns. He rented a massive house and filled it with friends and freeloaders, flipping shares like a real estate shark.

One summer break from college, he hooked me and a buddy up with a gig cleaning houses out there. The women who usually cleaned were hanging up their mops, and Uncle Larry convinced us to start a "business."

He did all the legwork. Signed up eight houses for $65 a pop. Five hundred bucks a week for two teenage idiots who barely knew which end of a vacuum to plug in. In the late '80s, that was baller money.

We'd ferry out on Tuesdays when the weekend crowds left, lug a beat-up red wagon full of cleaning supplies through the sand, and work for two days. At night, we'd crash at Larry's place, smoke his weed, drink his beer, and watch *The Pope of Greenwich Village* on loop. *"They got my thumb, Charlie. They got my thummmbbbb..."* Still a classic.

Cleaning wasn't exactly our calling. We sucked. I don't think I had ever actually cleaned *anything* before that summer. It felt like riding a unicycle drunk.

By noon, we'd already cracked open a six-pack of Keystone from Larry's fridge. By house two, we were stoned out of our minds. Damage was inevitable. By house three, all bets were off.

We walked through screen doors like confused Labradors. Smashed low-hanging chandeliers. Knocked over vases. Left the houses somehow dirtier than when we arrived. We covered up the evidence and blamed it on whoever rented the house before. Nobody ever asked questions.

Fire Island was wild back then—weed in every ashtray, used condoms abandoned like deflated balloon animals at a clown rave afterparty.

One time, we wandered into a house we thought was empty and found two half-drunk older women in the hot tub, smoking joints and sipping Zima—Zima was like if Sprite gave up on itself and joined a sorority. Totally gross. Totally unforgettable.

They asked if we wanted to join. When duty calls.

That summer was awesome.

.   .   .

When I graduated from college, I moved back home to save some cash, but the walls closed in fast. After four years of independence, sleeping in my old bedroom felt like being stuffed back into a womb I didn't fit in anymore.

My uncle made me an offer: Come live with him on the Upper East Side. Rent-free. The only catch? I had to save a set amount from every paycheck into an interest-bearing account he helped me open. It was one of the most important life lessons I ever got, even if I didn't know it at the time.

He taught me about savings accounts, stocks, bonds, mutual funds. He handed me the *Wall Street Journal* every morning like it was the Bible. I soaked it all up. Still love that stuff today. (If I had a do-over, I probably would have been a financial planner.)

Larry's apartment was classic New York—a railroad layout, exposed brick, wood floors, a kitchen-sized mouse problem, and cockroaches the size of remote-controlled cars.

They owned the kitchen.

You'd flip on the light at 2 a.m. and hear the tiny patter of insect feet scattering across the counters like they were late for a meeting.

The mice weren't much better.

One night I got up to get a glass of water and caught one hauling ass across the hallway like it was auditioning for *American Ninja Warrior.*

I grabbed the first thing I could—a big pot from the kitchen—and spent an hour stalking it around the apartment like I was Steve Irwin hunting a deranged croc.

When I finally trapped it under the pot, I slid a piece of cardboard underneath, carried it to the window, and launched the whole thing three stories down onto 86th Street.

Pretty sure it landed on a taxi, lit a cigarette, and kept going.

I learned pretty quick to sleep with my mouth closed.

At first, it was amazing. Freedom. Weed. Wings at 3 a.m. Movies any time you wanted. Bars on every corner. Hell, you could get a liverwurst sandwich at 4 in the morning in your bathrobe if you wanted.

Larry gave me his office as a room. Foldout couch. Accordion door that wouldn't close all the way. And his TV? Blasting at ungodly volumes all night because he'd pop out his hearing aids and just *vibe* on old westerns and '70s movies, half-naked, walking around in tighty-whities.

Living with him wasn't easy. He loved to talk. And talk. And talk. Every conversation started with, "Um, can I make a suggestion?" I loved him, but I loved silence too—and with Larry, silence was extinct.

Still, my friends loved him. Ray used to crash at the apartment constantly, stoned out of his mind. Larry would come home, see him snoring on the couch, and say, "Sleeping Beauty still breathing?"

For Larry's birthday one year, I wanted to get him something big to say thanks. Something heartfelt. You'd think: a nice watch, a cool jacket, maybe a good dinner.

Nope. I bought him the biggest glass bong I could find at the head shop down the street. Three feet tall. Red. Translucent. Glorious.

Larry laughed so hard when he opened it, then coughed so violently after his first hit that he puked in the sink. He never touched it again. Me and Ray, though? We put that thing to *work* like Cheech Marin had personally handed it to us and said, "Make me proud, vatos."

Larry also rode motorcycles—usually a beat-up Honda Shadow— with this full-body heated suit that made him look like an astronaut wired for demolition. His biker gang? The Chi Riders. Not exactly the Hells Angels. They sounded like they threatened people with guilt and pastrami.

Eventually, I moved out, got my own place. Larry stayed in that apartment forever—literally over forty years. Still paying $700 a month while the units around him went for $5,000. The owners of the building offered him half a million to move. He laughed and stayed. He was the last man standing in a building full of luxury gut renovations. He'd sneak into the empty apartments and do laundry in the brand-new washers, rotating so nobody would catch on. They broke the mold with him.

A few years ago, on my mom's birthday, Ronni and I had plans to see a Broadway show with friends. Nothing huge, just a night out.

But there was a problem. My mom hadn't heard from Larry in over a week.

That was... not possible. Not him. Larry never missed a birthday. Especially not my mom's. They spoke almost every day.

He loved to butcher "Happy Birthday" at the top of his lungs in that pitchy, off-key, deaf-guy warble we all secretly adored. If you sneezed within a twenty-mile radius, Larry would call to say, "Bless you."

At intermission, sitting in the theater, it hit me: *Something's wrong.*

I called my brother. "What do we do?" I asked.

He didn't hesitate. "You need to go to his apartment. Right now."

Ronni and I left the show, hailed a cab uptown. The ride felt like it took hours. I stared out the window, every worst-case scenario crowding into my chest, pressing down until I could barely breathe.

When we got to his building, we buzzed and buzzed. No answer. I called his cell. Called his landline. Nothing.

The building was empty except for him. No neighbors' doors to knock on. No one to ask.

That's when the fear really set in.

There was a phone number taped inside the foyer glass—for emergencies. I called it. It was the super, a guy who adored Larry like everyone else. When he picked up, I could hear it in his voice—he already knew something was wrong. He told me he hadn't seen Larry in days. He was all the way downtown, but he said he'd get dressed and be there as fast as he could.

We waited. And waited. The minutes dragging like hours.

Ronni was pacing. I was banging on the buzzer like an idiot, as if Larry would magically snap awake and answer.

When the super finally arrived, he let us in the building and we hurried up the three flights of stairs.

We got to his apartment but the super couldn't find the master key. We tried ringing the bell. Pounded on the door. Screamed Larry's name.

Nothing.

Then the super remembered: the apartment next door was still vacant and unlocked. He could climb out the window, onto the fire escape, and into Larry's place.

He went. I stayed in the hallway, heart hammering in my ears. Ronni grabbed my arm.

Minutes passed.

Then the super opened the door from inside.

His face said everything. He didn't have to say the words.

I said it anyway. "Is he in there?"

The super swallowed hard. "Yeah. I'm sorry. He passed. He's in his chair... looks like he's been there a while."


Everything tilted. The hallway, the floor, the walls—none of it made sense. Ronni started crying. I stood there stunned.

Not Uncle Larry. Not like this.

I called my brother. I could barely get the words out. He said he would call my mom. He didn't want me to have to break her heart on her birthday.

We called for an ambulance. And the morgue.

And then we just... waited.

Standing there in the hallway. In the stale bleach-and-bug-spray smell of that old building. Hearing sirens, hearing city noise, but feeling completely alone.

I kept thinking about how I hadn't visited enough. How I hadn't called enough. How he must have been alone, scared, maybe confused. And now he was gone.

The paramedics finally arrived.

They went inside. I followed but hesitated. I didn't want to see him like that. Before I could turn the corner, one of the paramedics asked if I could turn on a light. I fumbled through the kitchen looking for the switch, half expecting to see that same gaggle of roaches scurry across the counter.

Then, out of nowhere, one of them shouted:

*"HE'S ALIVE!"*

Huh? I couldn't believe what I was hearing.

I ran into the living room.

And there was Larry—laying in his chair in his underwear, blinking at everyone like *we* were the crazy ones.

The paramedics were shouting in his face, "Sir! Are you okay? Are you hurt?" Larry just looked at them, confused, and said:

"I was sleeping."

Jesus Christ. I turned to Ronni and yelled, "*HE'S ALIVE!*"

She screamed back from the hallway, "*HE'S ALIVE??*"

I called my brother and screamed into the phone, "*DUDE, HE'S ALIVE!*"

He shouted back, "*HE'S ALIVE???*"

We all started laughing. Laughing like lunatics. Laughing the way Larry would have if he could hear us properly.

But the story didn't end there.


Once the chaos settled, we realized something was really wrong. Larry looked frail. His skin hung off him. His eyes were foggy. He hadn't shaved or dressed in days.

Ronni found a piece of paper crumpled on the desk in his office. It was a doctor's report—from an oncologist.

We had no idea what any of it meant, so we sent a photo of it to my brother's wife, who's a physician assistant.

The answer came back like a hammer: Stage 4 lung cancer. Spread everywhere. And he'd had a series of mini-strokes.

He never told us. He didn't want anyone to worry. Classic Uncle Larry—trying to protect everyone else until the very end. He probably didn't want to put a damper on things. Or maybe he was in denial.

We moved fast after that.

We got him a live-in nurse. Scheduled appointments. Tried to make sense out of it all.

The whole thing was surreal.

But a week later, the nurse called at 5 a.m. Larry had fallen, hit his head, and wasn't moving.

When I got to the hospital, he was unconscious, already on life support. We moved him into hospice. He died a few hours later.

This time, for real.


The funeral was packed.

Friends from Fire Island. Old neighbors. People from the city.

Everyone had a story about Uncle Larry. Everyone had a memory that ended in laughter.

We buried him in his motorcycle jacket, a red schmata on his head, turquoise jewelry wrapped around his arms. Belt buckle shining. Helmet tucked under his arm. Ready for one last ride.

Before we put him in the ground, I played a recording on my phone: Larry laughing uncontrollably for two minutes straight at a holiday dinner years ago.

That's the last thing he gave us. That laugh. That light.

Wherever he is now, I hope it's just... Groovy.

# Switching Seats on the Titanic

My next job was different. It was a much larger operation—a well-known post-production shop with over a hundred employees, located in the Daily News Building on 42nd Street. Every time I walked through the main entrance, I felt like Peter Parker heading into the *Daily Bugle*.

It was the opposite of Gary's place in every way. No human feces on the steps (and if there were, someone else would have cleaned it up). Plenty of company merch—no more sweaty gym shirts for me. The building was so huge that if there were mice, they probably had their own wing.

The place was called Pixel Perfect. You had to be pretty damn confident—or crazy—to stick the word *Perfect* in your company name. Every time I said it, I heard it in a British accent. The place looked like a spaceship. Walking the halls felt like wandering the set of a *Star Trek* movie—people shuffling around with purpose, vanishing behind doors that led to mysterious, important rooms. They did it all: editing, visual effects, graphics, color correction, animation, audio.

When I first started working there, Johnny Depp and Kate Moss were on a project.

Kate Moss—my actual hall pass. I had a full-blown crush on her and somehow managed not to make an ass out of myself.

I even got Ronni Johnny Depp's autograph, like that made it less weird.

And then I rode the elevator with Bill Murray.

I mean, come on.

This wasn't Jack Klugman territory anymore. These people were rockstars—and I wanted to be around rockstars.

Even though I had some experience, no amount of time with Gary could've prepared me for the speed and intensity here. Producers barked orders. Artists barked back. Technical terms flew over my head like pigeons fleeing a subway rat. Suddenly, the fear kicked in hard. Part of me wished I was back cleaning up dead mice in Gary's sweaty shirt. At least there, the misery was predictable.

This was the New York Yankees versus the Bad News Bears.

I was hired by Lori—mid-thirties, ice-cold professional, not much of a people person. She ran the scheduling department like a general. There were five or six women, all younger than her—and me, the lone guy.

My job was simple: sit at a computer and schedule client sessions. Easy enough, right? I shadowed Shelly—tall, redheaded, freckled. She wasn't my type, but she was funny, sexy, laid-back—and insanely good at her job. They all were. They moved fast, talked faster, and took no shit from anyone.

And they ran the place. Whoever controlled the schedule controlled the artists—and the clients.

Because I wasn't there to hit on them like every other guy, they adopted me. Big sister energy. Protective. Encouraging. They saved my ass more times than I could count.

But this was the '90s, and office culture was... loose.

As we got more comfortable, the teasing crossed lines—only in one direction. Shoulder rubs. Back tickles. Ass pinches.

It was happening to *me*.

It was all out in the open—jokes, innuendos, wandering hands.

No HR seminars. No complaints. No lines drawn. It wasn't sinister —it was the culture.

Normal, even. At least, that's what I told myself.

After work, drinking became ritual. Bars were everywhere. It reminded me of college. It felt normal—part of the job. Take the edge off. Blend in. Be one of the guys.

Ronni had graduated and was living at home with her parents, coming into the city sometimes to stay with me. During the week, though, I was on my own.

One night out with the department, after too many drinks, one of the girls "accidentally" spilled an entire pint of beer on me. I brushed it off, laughing it away. Rookie mistake.

She dragged me into the bar bathroom, locked the door, and told me to take off my pants so she could dry them under the hand dryer.

I froze.

She stood there, waiting, smiling like it was no big deal. I looked at her the way a toddler looks at a parent who just asked them to drive the car.

I handed over my pants.

Standing there in my tighty-whities, on the dirty linoleum floor, I watched her crouch at the hand dryer, while I stood there feeling like a kid who'd peed his pants at a sleepover.

Ten minutes felt like ten years.

At some point, we both realized: this wasn't about drying my pants.

She tried. I didn't take the bait.

If it had been a few years earlier—pre-Ronni—maybe I would've been a different guy. But I was in love. Real love. It would've taken Kate Moss herself to even tempt me.

It wasn't until years later that I understood it for what it was: sexual harassment.

I didn't have those words back then.

It was just another blurry night.

Tossed into the trauma chest, saved for a rainy day.

The hammer finally dropped.

Lori called me in: "We need to have a serious talk."

My heart hit the floor.

She asked what I wanted to do with my career. I gave her the safe answer: producer. It sounded important. It sounded like a person who belonged here.

She barely nodded.

Scheduling wasn't working out.

I was being moved to another department.

One last shot.

If this didn't work, I was gone.

I'd almost gotten fired. At job number two.

That night, I sat at a bar alone, staring into a beer I didn't even want, living in the wreckage of a future that hadn't even happened yet.

The old soundtrack:

*You're a fraud. You're a screwup. You're not good enough.*

The next week, I started in Duplication.

The job was mindless—copying tapes, typing orders—but it was clean. No bullshit. No artifice. Just work.

And work, I could do.

My new boss, Lillian, was a tiny Italian New Yorker with the energy of a grenade. She yelled constantly. Ate constantly. Dropped crumbs and insults everywhere she went.

Working next to her was like standing next to a kitchen blender that never turned off.

But she loved me.

If you showed up and gave a shit, she loved you. And she told *everyone.* Loudly.

It fed something in me I didn't even realize was starving: Redemption. Validation. Respect.

I worked my ass off. Long hours. No complaints. No gossip. No excuses.

Not just for me—but for the version of me I wanted the world to see.

And it worked.

People noticed.

Other departments started pulling me in.

I started asking questions. Speaking up. Learning.

Lillian eventually hired a woman named Michelle to help with the growing workload.

At first, her nonstop talking drove me insane. But she was hilarious, wicked smart, and sharp as hell once she settled in. We hit it off—trauma bonding over Lillian's rage fits.

Michelle also liked to drink. Not a glass of wine. Whiskey. Jack and Coke.

She drank like a sailor, cursed like one, too.

And she never missed a beat at work.

We started going out after hours. First Thursdays. Then Fridays. Then Tuesdays, Wednesdays...

It was a slippery slope. Fast. Familiar. Fun—until it wasn't.

There was a bar around the corner called McBride's.

It became our second office.

Cheap beer, weed breaks, Counting Crows on the jukebox.

We laughed about work, about Lillian, about everything and nothing.

It was a mess. But it was ours.

Sometimes, the whole crew would migrate across town to the Port Authority bowling alley.

It was a dump—sticky floors, broken pins, toilets you needed a tetanus shot to use.

One night at the bowling alley, drunk off our asses, I stumbled into the bathroom and found a guy from work doing lines of coke off the back of a toilet tank.

He offered me a bump.

I didn't hesitate.

It wasn't my first time—and it wouldn't be my last.

The drinking.

The smoking.

The coke.

It all became part of the job. Part of the lifestyle.

A survival skill, I told myself.

Essential networking.

Then came the Circle Line Cruise.

A staff party. Big boat. Open bar.

Unlimited shots.

No supervision.

No off switch.

I blacked out fast.

The next thing I barely remembered—or rather, what I was told later —was that I walked up to the most respected senior editor in the company, in front of a crowd of people, and patted his belly.

Like a fucking golden retriever.

And then I made a crack about him gaining weight.

Loudly.

Drunkenly.

Obliviously.

Time froze.

The room went silent.

He didn't say a word.

He just stared at me.

The kind of look that could turn a human being into ash.

Someone yanked me away before I could finish digging my grave.

The next day, he called me into his edit suite.

"Do that again," he said, "and you're done here."

I apologized a hundred times. I meant every word. But it didn't matter.

I wasn't just embarrassed—I was mortified.

I didn't belong here. I was an impostor. A drunk. A joke.

And just like camp, just like always, I ran.

I took a job at a smaller shop.

Told myself it was a better opportunity.

Told myself it was growth.

But deep down, I knew: It was punishment.

Because no matter how far I ran, the shame always packed itself and came along for the ride.

What I didn't know then:

Pixel Perfect wasn't done with me yet.

Not even close. It would later give me the biggest opportunity of my career.

But for now, I was just switching seats on the *Titanic*.

# The Great Mind Fuck

When the call for my newest gig came in, it was from my old buddy Bobby. He was the first person I met at Gary's shop and became a good friend. Even though he was older, I always looked at him like a little brother. We used to laugh so hard we could've shit ourselves.

Bobby was about five feet six inches, 135 pounds, and had full Peter Brady energy—like that episode where he tries to date two girls at once. All confidence, no plan, and no clue.

One night, back when we were still working at Gary's place, a bunch of us went out for drinks. On the way, we stopped at an ATM. It was one of those vestibules with a glass front and a heater, so people waiting for the bus would sometimes hang out in there to stay warm.

That night, a woman was sitting in the corner, arms crossed, clearly not in a good mood. She had that look in her eye—the one that says, *Try me, motherfucker. Please.* Meanwhile, we were being loud as hell —laughing, cracking jokes, acting like idiots.

Bobby spotted a copy of the *Village Voice*—the classic downtown paper with concert listings, movie reviews, and a back section full of unapologetically unhinged personal ads. Naturally, he started reading them out loud, doing voices, putting on a show like he was auditioning for *SNL*.

Then he hit one that said: "Man seeks woman open to cross-dressing, light bondage and role play. Let's start with brunch."

We were already groaning when the woman in the corner stood up and started walking toward him.

Bobby, not reading the room at all, turned to her with a dumb grin and said: "Do you like brunch?"

What happened next wasn't a fight—it was WrestleMania in a fishbowl. She *unleashed*—purse swinging, fists flying, legs kicking. "You little motherfucker! I'm gonna kill you!"

Bobby dropped to the floor like a sandbag. The rest of us stood there, frozen, watching the chaos like we were watching two orangutans fornicating at the zoo. Horrified. Fascinated. Not entirely sure if we should intervene or let nature take its course.

Eventually, she either ran out of steam or spotted her bus, because she screamed one last time and stormed out into the night.

When it was over, Bobby was in a pile—ripped shirt, bleeding, scratched up like he'd been in a bar fight with a bobcat.

We just stared at him, then absolutely lost it. Laughed until our ribs hurt. It was either that or cry.

We hauled him back to the office, grabbing wine coolers and gauze pads on the way, and spent the rest of the night reenacting the whole thing like it was a war story—slow-motion kicks, dramatic sound effects, Bobby's cries for help. It was extremely therapeutic—for us. Not so much for Bobby.

The next day, we told him he had to go back to the bank and ask for the security footage—just in case he wanted to press charges. But let's be honest: We didn't care about justice. We just wanted to see the tape.

And holy shit—we got it. It was gold. Like *America's Funniest Home Videos* if it were hosted by Randy "Macho Man" Savage. Fucking Bobby. I love that guy.

When he left for a new job, it left a void. Even though he'd been there longer, I admired the drive he had to move his career forward. He wound up at a place called Damarc Studios. Cute—named after the founders, Damon and Marc.

They weren't particularly big anymore, but they were famous. Damon and Marc had done one of the most famous music videos of the '80s—a groundbreaking piece that shattered barriers in visual effects. They were pioneers. Legends.

By the time I got there, Marc was long gone. Damon was the king of the castle now, and it was a dictatorship.

He was brilliant. No question. Creative in ways most people couldn't even comprehend. He could see things on a screen nobody else could see. But he was also terrifying.

Damon looked like he belonged at a Velvet Underground afterparty —good-looking, wild dresser, top hat and tux jacket one day, cargo shorts the next. He totally rocked it. The only questionable choice was the ponytail clinging to a receding hairline. A battle long lost.

There was the famous story of Damon arguing with a client over a commercial. When the client refused to budge, Damon walked out, dragged the UPS guy delivering a package into the edit suite, showed him the spot, and asked what stood out. The UPS guy pointed out the exact issue Damon had been fighting about. Without saying a word, Damon looked at the client, and the client sank into his chair like a scolded puppy.

It was the coolest fucking thing I'd ever seen.

Being around Damon was like standing next to a caged tiger. Most days, he just paced behind the bars. But you never forgot that if the door ever opened—even a little—he would tear your throat out.

And that was only half the story.

The other half was the version of Damon who made you feel like a king.

He'd hand out absurd gifts for no reason. Throw lavish summer parties in the Hamptons for the whole staff. Toast every employee like they were a war hero. He could be generous, charming, disarming.

You never knew which Damon you were going to get.

The one who made you feel special—or the one who made you wish you didn't exist.

That whiplash was what kept you hooked. That sickness was what kept you silent.

I got hired to work the front desk as a coordinator. $36,000 a year. A big jump from the $20K I made at Pixel Perfect. Now I could save up for my own place—and for a ring. But $5,000 for an engagement ring? It might as well have been $5 million at that point. But I was determined.

If I thought Pixel Perfect was fast-paced, Damarc Studios made that look like a lazy river at Six Flags. It was a war zone.

Damon's standards weren't just high.

They were *impossible*.

Everyone walked on eggshells. All day. Every day.

By my second morning, I knew:

I had made one of the worst decisions of my life.

My direct supervisor was Jerry—ten years older, a lifer. Everyone there seemed to have worked there ten, fifteen, even twenty years. Like prisoners with really good dental plans.

Jerry was hilarious—a former cruise ship entertainer turned control freak. He was neat to the point of obsession. Nothing could ever be changed. Not because it was the best way—but because it was *Damon's* way.

He told me my first week on the job, "If you work hard, one day you'll have my job."

He stayed another fifteen years.

Jerry loved bossing me around. Until Damon ripped him a new asshole in front of everyone. Then he'd grunt, pull up his sagging pants, and storm off down the hall like a wounded duck.

Funny. And sad.

Over time, I realized: at Damarc, the bigger your title, the bigger the target on your back.

One weekend, after working almost twenty-four hours straight with no break, I was minding my business at the front desk when I heard a huge crash and Damon screaming.

Before I could even stand up, he came barreling down the hall— broken chair in hand—and threw it full force at my head.

It missed me by an inch.

Almost shattered the window behind me.

Without missing a beat, he screamed, "PUT THAT FUCKING CHAIR IN CONNELLY'S OFFICE!"

I liked Connelly. He was the studio manager—a funny Detroit guy who looked like a cartoon version of Robert Redford. Always wore shirts two sizes too big, wrinkled khakis, and a tie. The only person in the building who wore one. Like it gave him a shred of self-respect.

When Damon screamed at him that Monday—for the broken chair he didn't even break—Connelly just straightened his tie and asked me how my day was going.

*What the actual fuck?*

Despite all this, I worked my ass off. And I was rewarded.

Promoted to producer.

$42,000 a year.

It felt huge.

It felt like I could finally tell Ronni what I made without cringing.

It felt like I was somebody.

Connelly and I even became friends—hockey games, heavy drinking, real trust.

He became my first mentor.

He made me believe I could do more—maybe even run my own company one day.

But Damarc had a way of revealing everyone's rot.

One night, working late, Connelly wandered over and stood silently in front of my desk.

Creepy.

I was about to ask if he was having a stroke when I saw it:

His balls, hanging out through his zipper like some grotesque, half-deflated balloon animal.

My mentor.

Laughing his ass off as he walked away.

At Damarc, the line between prank and harassment was a dotted one —and always shifting.

At first, I escaped Damon's direct wrath.

Too junior to bother with.

But part of me *wanted* the challenge.

I thought maybe—just maybe—my people skills would win him over.

Maybe he'd see something in me.

Maybe we'd be buddies.

No. We would not be buddies.

Fridays were fear factories.

Five o'clock rolled around, and you practically hid under your desk. Someone always got tapped to work the weekend.

One night, after finally closing up at 11 p.m., Ronni was waiting downstairs in the car. A rare weekend off—a tiny miracle.

I was about to leave when the phone rang.

*Fuck.*

I shouldn't have answered.

I answered.

It was Damon.

No greeting.

No recognition.

Just a Chinese food order barked at me like I was a voicemail.

Mr. Chang's. An hour. Bring it to his place.

It was going to be 3 a.m. before I got home.

Ronni was waiting outside.

I locked up.

Got in the car.

Before I could speak, Ronni said, "What did Damon do now?"

We picked up $1,000 worth of Chinese food and drove across town to The San Remo.

Yes—The San Remo. One of the most iconic apartment buildings in New York. Where Bono lived. Where Steve Martin lived. Where Damon had a duplex.

When I got upstairs, he was jamming with his wannabe Beatles band.

Smoke everywhere. Drinks everywhere. Music blasting.

He was thrilled to see me. Like I was a buddy who just stopped by.

I sat there for hours, eating dumplings, listening to their awful music, while Ronni waited in the car downstairs until almost 3 a.m.

You can't make this shit up.


When I finally got assigned to a job with Damon, it was a pro bono spot for some nonprofit. Of course it was.

A "free" job.

You'd think that would be easy.

You'd be wrong.

Damon threw the kitchen sink at it.

Twenty-hour days.

Three days straight with no sleep.

No mercy. No forgiveness.

And he wasn't even there.

He was flying the fucking Concorde to Paris every weekend to see his girlfriend.

One weekend, after I'd worked thirty-six straight hours on the project, Damon called to check in.

Speakerphone, as usual—so he could yell at everyone at once.

He asked about the budget.

I gave him the numbers I had.

Hearing how much money we'd burned on a pro bono job made him lose his fucking mind.

He screamed.

Spit rage through the speaker.

Ripped me to shreds.

And without thinking—

I hung up.

The room went silent.

Phone rang again.

More screaming.

I hung up again.

Phone rang a third time.

This time—a different voice.

"DON'T HANG UP," he said.

Not screaming.

Not furious.

*Just different.*

He apologized.

Said he'd had a fight with his girlfriend.

Said he took it out on us.

Thanked us.

Told us to finish up and go home.

We hung up, stunned.

Maybe—finally—I'd cracked the monster.

Monday morning, I stepped off the elevator feeling uneasy.

Connelly was waiting.

Said, "Come with me."

He led me into a back edit room.

Damon was already there.

Staring.

Connelly did the talking.

I was made to recount everything that had happened.

Out loud.

In front of Damon.

Connelly said that what I had done was unacceptable.

Disrespectful.

That I had undermined authority.

That I had created chaos.

Damon never spoke.

Never blinked.

I left feeling hollow.

Like someone had scooped my guts out with a spoon.

That day, I decided I was done.

I cleared my desk.

Took down my photos of Ronni.

My coffee mug.

My stupid pens.

I left the office.

Dead man walking.

And for the first time, I didn't feel lucky to have escaped.

I felt ashamed for ever thinking I needed to stay.

I made a promise to myself that day:

*If I ever have my own company, I will never treat people that way.*

# Anchovies and the Not-So-Elusive Smiley Face

When I was at Pixel Perfect, it was way more corporate than Gary's place.

There was a CEO—Paula Denton—who moved through the halls like a human audit.

Pantsuit, short haircut, barely said a word.

People were terrified of her.

In a business built on chaos and creativity, she felt like an accountant lost at Burning Man.

She didn't belong.

But that made her even more important.

Because getting noticed by someone like that meant you really mattered.

And that's all I ever really wanted—to matter.

I wasn't the kind of person who got intimidated by authority.

I saw it as a challenge.

A game.

If everyone else scattered when she walked by, maybe that was the exact moment to lean in.

One of the only ways you ever heard from her was through company-wide emails.

Policy changes, revenue reports—cold stuff.

But every once in a while, she'd send out a different kind of message —a congratulations to someone who had "gone above and beyond."

With it came a literal smiley face printed on yellow paper, left on your desk with a signed letter from Paula.

It sounded stupid.

Maybe it was stupid.

But it wasn't stupid to me.

It was proof.

Proof that someone at the top had seen me.

I wanted that smiley face.

I wanted it bad.

Not for the prize.

Not for the politics.

But because a part of me—a deep, quiet part—still believed that if I worked hard enough, if I paid attention to the right details, I could be one of the special ones.

Work hard? Sure. Everyone did that.

But watch harder—that's where the advantage was.

Once a month they held Pizza Friday—management's idea of "culture."

Most people made a mad dash for the pepperoni and veggie pies.

But I noticed something different:

There was always one anchovy pizza.

And nobody touched it.

Except Paula Denton.

Every month, she made a beeline for the anchovies, like clockwork.

These were the things I picked up on.

The little cracks where you could wedge a conversation.

The openings everyone else missed.

I had read *How to Win Friends and Influence People* and *The Prince* by Machiavelli in my early twenties.

Not exactly beach reading—but I wasn't interested in doing things the easy way.

Carnegie taught me that people mostly wanted to talk about themselves.

Machiavelli taught me that survival wasn't about brute force—it was about perception.

Both lessons stuck.

The next Pizza Friday, I made my move.

I timed it perfectly.

As she reached for the anchovy slice, so did I.

Boom.

Instant icebreaker.

We ended up talking about anchovies for five minutes before I even told her my name.

Then we talked for almost an hour—about the company, her day-to-day, the things that made her tick.

And yeah—about me too.

Not bragging.

Just planting the seed.

All because of fucking anchovies.

And guess what?

The next month, there it was—a yellow smiley face waiting on my desk.

Signed by Paula Denton herself.

It wasn't just a piece of paper.

It was proof that I could find my way in.

That if I played it right—if I worked, watched, and listened—I could be seen.

Maybe even be special.

That's how I approached work.

That's how I approached people.

That's how I survived.

Even if deep down, part of me was terrified that if anyone ever really looked too closely—

They'd realize I wasn't special at all.

Maybe that's why I noticed the anchovy pizza.

Nobody wanted it.

Nobody saw the point of it.

Except the ones who knew better.

Same with me.

# How to Win Friends and Influence People—Like the Prince

I learned early that if you played the part well enough, people didn't just notice—

they applauded.

Fifth grade.

School play.

*The King and I.*

I was cast as Prince Chulalongkorn—the boy king who bows, smiles, says his lines just right.

All I wanted was to get it perfect.

To stand in the right place.

Say the right thing.

Make them believe.

When the curtain fell, they clapped.

They clapped for me.

And somewhere deep down, even at that age, I tucked away the lesson:

Play the role. Play it well enough—and they'll give you the crown.

I'd survived Damarc and Damon.

I needed a reset.

I needed a win.

I needed a way out.

Then Pixel Perfect called.

They wanted me to come back.

This time it wouldn't be with Lillian in duplication. It was more responsibility. More exposure. More opportunity.

They needed a producer, and they wanted to see if I would be interested. I jumped at it. It wasn't just the chance to escape Damon and the chaos of Damarc. It was a chance at redemption. My triumphant return. They needed me. It felt really good.

By then, Ronni and I were living together.

First apartment.

First real shot at building something stable.

She had a regular schedule—a teacher's life—home by 3:30, dinner plans, routines.

And I had chaos.

At first, it felt like we could balance it.

She had her world. I had mine.

But the more serious my work got, the more I started choosing it over her. Over us.

Late nights. Missed plans.

Coming home drunk, or worse, coming home physically sober but mentally still sitting on a conference call somewhere.

Every time work needed me, I said yes.

Every time Ronni asked if I'd be home for dinner, I said probably—and almost never was.

It wasn't that I didn't love her.

I did.

But the gravitational pull of being needed, of being important—

it was stronger than anything waiting behind our front door.

I was still playing the part.

And for the first time, I was starting to lose track of who I was playing it for.

Most of the people I used to know at the office had moved on. The girls from scheduling were gone, and Michelle had left shortly after I did.

New faces, new politics, new games to learn.

In a lot of ways, I was starting over.

And I knew better than anyone that you didn't get many second chances in this business.

So I went to work.

Hard.

Head down, no complaints, no attitude.

Just results.

I wasn't trying to be flashy.

I wasn't trying to be anyone's buddy.

I was trying to prove that they'd been right to bring me back.

In a business built on chaos, missed deadlines, and blown budgets, I became the guy you could trust.

Projects got done.

Clients were happy.

Problems disappeared before anyone knew they existed.

I wasn't making noise.

I was making momentum.

And momentum has a way of attracting attention.

That's when Courtney Mason noticed me.

Courtney ran the sales department—and when I say "ran," I mean she was the sales department.

Courtney wasn't just a rainmaker—she was a fucking monsoon.

She could sell sand in the desert and make you feel lucky to get a handful.

Funny, self-deprecating, sharp as hell.

People flocked to her.

If you were on her good side, you were golden.

If you weren't, you were invisible.

Exactly the kind of person I wanted—no, needed—to notice me.

It didn't take long.

Within two months, Courtney made it clear:

I was the only producer she wanted working with her clients.

No questions. No arguments.

She started introducing me like a prizefighter.

"This is Jason—the only guy I trust with my clients. If he's on your project, you're in good hands."

She'd say it in boardrooms, bars, lunches, late-night calls.

She built my reputation before I even had time to earn it.

And I played the part.

God, I played it hard.

I stayed late.

I worked weekends.

Even when I didn't have anything real to do, I made sure to bump into her in the halls at 2 a.m., hoping for a casual conversation, a glass of wine, a new piece of insider knowledge.

I became her shadow.

Her fixer.

Her guy.

And after a while, it wasn't just meetings and handshakes.

It was rides home in her BMW at 2 a.m. While everyone else from the office slogged onto the subway or the Long Island Railroad, I was getting door-to-door service from the most respected person at the company.

We'd sit outside my apartment smoking cigarettes, talking business, talking life.

Sometimes for thirty minutes, an hour.

I'd see the lights flick on behind the curtains.

Ronni, peeking out the window, wondering what the hell I was still doing out there.

But to me, it wasn't just a ride.

It was a coronation.

Courtney wasn't just handing me business skills—she was handing me an identity.

And I wore it like armor.

She even invited Ronni and me to her son's bar mitzvah—something that didn't happen for just anyone at Pixel Perfect.

It wasn't just a bar mitzvah.

It was a full-blown spectacle.

Arcade games everywhere.

Photo booth.

DJ.

A famous basketball player even recorded a personalized message for the bar mitzvah boy.

A full bar for the adults.

Celebrity impersonators drifting around like lost extras from a Vegas revue.

A three-course meal served on china that probably cost more than my first car.

It felt less like a coming-of-age party and more like the royal wedding.

I thought back to my own bar mitzvah that took place in the back ballroom of a local Jewish delicatessen—not many people, not many close friends, just a bunch of old relatives dancing like it was their last night on earth while I clung to a folding chair for dear life during the hora.

The whole place smelled like cold cuts and pickles.

It wasn't fancy, but it was mine.


Standing there, half-drunk on free champagne, I didn't just want to be invited to her world.

I wanted to live there.

I didn't want the spectacle.

I wanted the power.

The money.

The success.

And more than anything, I wanted Ronni to see it, too—

to believe I could get it for us.

Even if, deep down, I wasn't sure I could.

I wasn't just her producer.

I was part of her circle now.

I was becoming someone.

One of the biggest lessons Courtney gave me was deceptively simple:

*"Never say no to a client,"* she told me.

*"You're not selling a service. You're selling you. You're the reason they come back."*

I took it all to heart.

Every word.

Every drink.

And that's the thing—the drinking started to come with it.

Not pounding shots at the bar—not yet.

But casual drinks with clients.

Glasses of wine in the office.

Martinis at dinner meetings.

Champagne to celebrate a pitch win.

At first, it didn't even feel like drinking.

It felt like playing the part.

Like polishing the armor.

A drink at lunch?

Client culture.

A glass of wine at the desk?

Team bonding.

A few beers after hours?

Relationship building.

I wasn't some sloppy mess—I was thriving.

I was getting closer to the center of power, closer to the real players.

And if it meant drinking during the week, if it meant blurring the lines between work and home, so be it.

The truth was, by then, drinking wasn't just something I did at home anymore or with work buddies at some dive bar.

It was becoming part of the costume.

Part of what made me "fit."

And I didn't question it.

Because it was working.

And just when it seemed like I'd found my lane—

Courtney pulled me into something even bigger.

She had a friend from the business named Eli.

Eli was a consultant—the kind of guy companies brought in when they needed to grow fast or start something new.

He was well known for launching one of the most successful editing companies in the industry several years back—and he was still making a living off that reputation, even though he hadn't built anything new in a while.

But Eli had a sharp eye for talent—and a sharp memory for the people who had helped him along the way.

Back when Eli launched his first company, Courtney had been a huge part of it—landing him one of his biggest early clients, a cornerstone of his early success.

They trusted each other.

They spoke the same language: business, loyalty, survival.

When Eli came to her about Ingrid, it wasn't just a favor.

It was a plan.

Ingrid was a rising star—a brilliant editor, opinionated, fiercely loyal to her clients—but still freelance, still untethered.

Eli wanted to give her a home base—a room at Pixel Perfect where she could start anchoring her business, build momentum, and eventually break off into a full boutique downtown.

At the same time, it would boost Pixel Perfect's reputation—bringing in better talent, better clients, and a little downtown credibility they didn't have yet.

It was smart all the way around.

At the time, I had already been producing a few jobs for Ingrid and her clients.

And just like Courtney, Ingrid and Eli made it clear—they wanted only me dealing with their people.

I started getting closer to them—working late, hanging out, quietly becoming part of their circle.

Ingrid didn't work like the rest of the place.

Her edit bay was a fortress—not because she was cold, but because she didn't do small talk.

With clients, she was electric—commanding, funny, confident.

She could juggle a conference call, an edit session, and a last-minute dinner reservation without breaking a sweat.

But around the rest of the staff—the producers, the techs, the other editors—it got awkward fast.

Hanging out by the water cooler wasn't her thing.

She was tall—over six feet—and she carried herself like it.

Not just physically, but in a way that made people instinctively keep their distance.

Not rude.

Just... big.

A presence.

Most people steered clear.

I didn't.

I went in.

I asked questions.

I figured out what she needed before she had to ask.

I didn't treat her like she was scary.

I treated her like she was part of the team—even if most days she wasn't.

And that became a quiet edge for me.

Where other people saw difficult or demanding,

I saw opportunity.

I wasn't just surviving those tough rooms anymore.

I was starting to make them my niche.

When the time came for Eli and Ingrid to finally open up the new shop downtown, they needed someone to run it.

Someone who could balance Ingrid's highwire intensity.

Someone who could keep clients happy, keep the engine running, and build the business from scratch.

They needed me.

Courtney.

Eli.

Ingrid.

They all agreed:

I was the guy.

Executive producer.

At the new company we were about to launch: Prime Cut.

I was finally stepping into the big leagues.

Running the show.

Building something real.

It was everything I wanted.

Everything I thought I needed.

I wasn't just playing the part anymore. I was becoming it.

# Still Zero?

Opening Prime Cut was supposed to be my arrival.

My first real taste of accountability.

My first real chance to stand out.

My first real shot at being *somebody*.

I'd always worked hard—showed up, smiled, bled loyalty—but this was different.

This time, Courtney, Eli, and Ingrid were counting on me.

Not for a favor, or a ride to the dentist, or a base hit in some beer league softball game. This time, the stakes were higher.

They needed me to build something.

To *be* something.

And under all that excitement, there was a darker undercurrent I didn't fully understand yet:

Prove it.

Prove it to Gary.

Prove it to Damon.

Prove it to Jolie.

Prove it to my dad.

Prove it to everyone who made me feel like I wasn't good enough.

I thought it was just ambition.

Really, it was a wound.

We found a small space near Union Square.

Old bones. High ceilings. Elevator that sounded like it was gasping for breath.

But it had charm. Downtown energy. Cooler restaurants. Cooler everything.

We built it from scratch—phones, electricity, floors, paint.

It wasn't mine—not on paper.

But I treated it like it was.

Every late night. Every ounce of energy.

Everything that should have gone to Ronni.

Or maybe even to myself.

But that's how it had to be.

If I wanted them to thank their lucky stars they picked me.

The new space was beautiful.

Bright. Colorful. Tasteful.

Ingrid had a hell of an eye for design.

It looked like an art gallery and a boutique hotel had a one-night stand.

And for the first time, I had my own office.

Not just a desk wedged in an oversized utility closet.

A real office.

With a fancy area rug. The kind of rug you don't buy until you believe you deserve nice things.

They gave me a raise—small, a little insulting—but I didn't complain.

Negotiating for myself?

Forget it.

I could haggle a flea market vendor out of his last concert tee, but when it came to my own salary, I folded like a lawn chair at a barbecue.

The work started pouring in.

We booked job after job.

Built real momentum.

For the first six months, we were a rocket ship.

Pixel Perfect couldn't praise us enough.

We became their golden goose—the gift that kept on giving.

And with success came freedom.

Weekly yoga classes for clients.

Wine and cheese afterward.

Swag, parties, downtown clout.

I stocked the place with wine, under the very legitimate excuse of "client hospitality."

Two cases turned into six.

Wine turned into beer.

Beer turned into vodka, tequila, rum—whatever I felt like ordering that week.

Prime Cut became less an office and more a speakeasy with big screens.

We entertained like pros.

Built real relationships—or at least ones that felt real after a few glasses of cabernet.

Tom was one of those clients—a hilarious, high-level executive producer who could drink, joke, and hold court with the best of them.

One night, Tom and his husband invited us to their penthouse for martinis before dinner.

I wasn't really a martini guy, but turning down a drink felt illegal.

By the time we stumbled out the door, I could barely see straight.

Somewhere between the laughter and the drinks, dinner happened—and so did the slow, hilarious realization that Ingrid—plastered—had somehow snuck her foot into Tom's lap.

Tom, being both generous and extremely gay, gave me a subtle "help me" nod.

I distracted Ingrid long enough for him to move his chair and preserve everyone's dignity.

Typical night.

There was another weekend when Tom invited us (plus Ronni) to his Hamptons house for a pajama party.

He demanded we bring our "most fabulous" pajamas.

I showed up in navy blue pajamas with glow-in-the-dark stars.

Because, professionalism.

At some point—half-drunk, full-bellied—I went to use the bathroom on the other side of the house.

And promptly got *locked inside.*

I jiggled the handle, banged on the door, shouted. Nothing.

Finally, after what felt like an hour, I heard Ronni's voice calling.

I screamed back.

She came running—with Tom and his husband trailing behind her, laughing so hard they could barely breathe.

The door wouldn't budge.

But Tom, ever resourceful, stuck his head through the tiny bathroom window—and handed me a full glass of wine.

Because when life locks you in a bathroom, you still deserve a drink.


Meanwhile, back at work, the floor was cracking under us.

Pixel Perfect—the parent company—was bleeding money.

Layoffs. Rumors. Blood in the water.

They sent in a cost consultant: a corporate hatchet man in a suit.

He smiled. Complimented us.

Then gutted everything we'd built.

No more yoga.

No more parties.

No more fancy dinners with clients.

We warned him it would kill the business.

He didn't listen.

Sure enough, work dried up almost overnight.

Clients heard the rumors that Pixel might fold—and nobody wants their projects caught inside a collapsing circus tent.

One day, the cost consultant sat us down and asked, "What's booked next month?"

I said, deadpan:

"Zero."

He blinked. "Zero?"

"Yep. Zero."

"And the month after?"

"Still zero."

He asked for a six-month projection.

Ingrid and I burst out laughing.

"Still zero," I said.

It became a running joke for days:

Passing each other in the hallway, whispering, *Still zero?*

*Still zero.*

Laughter was the only thing keeping us from losing our minds.

Meanwhile, Ronni and I had been planning a trip.

Ten days in Italy.

Florence. Rome. Venice.

Pasta-making classes. Wine tastings. Gondolas.

Her dream trip.

Our escape.

The one thing—maybe the only thing—that was supposed to be just *ours*.

And then Pixel Perfect called me down to the main office.

They told me they'd found a buyer.

Someone who could save the company.

Someone who wanted Prime Cut.

Only catch?

They wanted me.

Not Ingrid.

She was too expensive.

Too much baggage.

But me?

I was the one salvageable thing they could build around.

They needed me at the buyer meeting.

I told them about Italy.

They told me how important this was.

How much was riding on it.

How I couldn't afford to miss it.

I went home that night and told Ronni.

I told her we had to cancel.

That this was bigger than both of us.

At first, she thought I was kidding.

She waited for me to laugh, to say, *Gotcha!*

Then she saw my face.

She crumbled.

I watched her hope collapse in front of me—and I didn't know how to fix it.

I tried to explain.

How important it was.

How much pressure I was under.

How I had no choice.

She didn't say much.

She didn't scream.

She just looked at me with a sadness that was worse than any fight we ever had.

And in my heart, I knew:

I was choosing work over love.

Again.

And the worst part?

At the time, I thought I was doing the right thing.

And honestly?

She never really let me forget it.

Thirty years later, if you mention Italy at the wrong moment, she'll still give me a look that could slice marble.

And I'll still deserve it.

The buyer came.

Slimy. Sleazy. Calculated.

First thing he did was pick up a framed photo of Ronni from my desk and call her my "trophy wife."

I knew, in that exact moment, I had made the wrong choice.

Canceling Italy.

Choosing work over love.

Choosing ambition over loyalty.

The whole thing was rotten.

They wanted me to betray Ingrid.

They wanted me to sell her out.

I sat there that afternoon drinking vodka and Diet Coke, trying to numb the sick feeling in my gut.

I'd sold out for nothing.

That's when Eli called.

Almost like he *knew*.

He said he'd heard rumors.

He offered me a lifeline—a new job, a fresh start, a way out.

He didn't just offer me a better salary.

He offered me a piece of my soul back.

Eli had given me Prime Cut.

Now, at another crossroads, he was giving me another shot.

For someone like him to trust me twice—that meant everything.

When I told Ingrid I was leaving, she was furious.

She thought I was abandoning her.

Maybe I was.

But better she be angry than know how close I came to betraying her.

Better she think I chased a better opportunity than realize how much pressure I'd been under to sell her out.

Walking away from Prime Cut hurt like hell.

Not because I loved it.

Because it showed me exactly how much of myself I was willing to trade just to feel important.

I thought if I built enough, mattered enough, won enough...

the emptiness would finally disappear.

It never did.

Regret's a quiet kind of poison. You don't even notice it spreading—

until someone hands you the antidote.

That someone was Eli.

# The Sky Is Falling

I wasn't looking for a new home. I was still dragging the weight of Prime Cut behind me, trying not to look back.

Eli and I met at a bar and he told me he was helping out a once-legendary studio that had hit the skids. Emerald had the name, the history, but the place was bleeding out. Bad management. No talent retention. And hovering over all of it was the founder—Magnus Thorne.

Magnus had a reputation. Groundbreaking director. Visionary, if you listened to the myth. But most people just gave you that BEWARE OF DOG look when his name came up. Eli said he wasn't directing much anymore, which meant he was way more involved at the studio—and not in a good way. "Eccentric," Eli called him. "Stubborn." That's the kind of language people use when they're trying to put a bow on a bomb.

But I'd worked with Damon. Compared with him, Magnus sounded like a Girl Scout with a juice box.

I wasn't intimidated. Hesitant, sure, but not scared. Eli had always seen me clearly—for what I was good at and what I could handle. He wanted me to come in as executive producer. It was a step up, and he made it worth my while. Doubled my salary. Six figures before thirty —another goal checked off the list.

When I met Magnus it was just a formality. He was charming enough. A little twitchy. Couldn't sit still. Bounced on the balls of his feet like a boxer before a fight—or a kid who had to pee. He ended our conversation like someone had flipped a switch and launched him out of the room. I clocked it. Nervous energy. Filed it away. Eli brushed it off, told me Magnus was brilliant. "Creative genius." It always amazes me how often that phrase is used to excuse people acting like assholes.

I started in July 2001. Summer was slow, which was fine with me. Gave me time to get to know the team and figure out how broken things really were. The staff was pretty good, a few toxic cliques, but nothing unmanageable. I sat in the producer pit instead of taking an office—wanted to lead from the front. Let people know I wasn't a helicopter boss, but I wasn't a pushover either. Fair but no bullshit. That was my style.

The place had no real stars, just serviceable people, which wasn't gonna cut it. I ended the "summer Fridays" thing when half the staff didn't show up my first week. I was used to working fifteen-hour days. We weren't a bank. I brought in three solid jobs early on— clients who'd never worked with Emerald before. It helped. The place had been dormant for months. When Eli showed me the books, I realized just how close to the edge we were. A few missed months and the whole thing would collapse. But I fed off that pressure. I was built for it.

Ronni and I were living in an apartment in Queens. I was working late. We didn't see much of each other, but she was always supportive. Especially with real money coming in. We were saving for a house. Talking about kids. Everything felt like it was finally lining up.

Then came the day that broke the world.

September 11 started like any other morning.

I took the charter bus into Manhattan, same as always. I think I saw smoke as we were entering the Midtown Tunnel—just a wisp in the sky, maybe. A few whispers between people who had noticed. Could've been construction. Could've been nothing. I don't really remember where the bus let me off, but it wasn't far from the office.

The city still felt like the city. That same pulse. That same rhythm. I walked the few blocks to Emerald, past bagel shops and newsstands, into the office. I was usually the first one in. The only person who ever beat me was Zack—our FX guy. He was always in early, always had the TV on in his suite at the end of the railroad hallway. I yelled out my usual hello and heard him shout for me to come back.

His voice didn't sound normal.

When I got there, he was staring at the screen.

"A plane hit the tower," he said, pointing. "They think it was an accident."

We both stared at the TV. One tower was on fire. Black smoke curling into a blue sky. It didn't feel real. Even the newscasters didn't know what to say. You could hear it in their voices—trying to fill airtime with speculation that felt thin and shaky.

I sat down next to Zack.

And then, while we were still trying to make sense of the first one, the second plane hit.

It tore across the screen like a silver bullet and disappeared into the second tower, followed by a massive fireball. Gasps erupted from the anchors. Someone screamed off-camera. The camera tilted, almost like the cameraman had flinched. Zack and I didn't move. We didn't speak. It was like time stopped.

In that moment, everything changed.

There was no more maybe. No accident. No question.

This was intentional. We were under attack, and we were in the warzone.

We sat frozen for what felt like hours—though it was probably just minutes—staring at the screen. People started trickling into the office. One by one, we heard the sound of the elevator ding, and they stepped into this new world we didn't yet understand.

Most of them had seen the smoke. None of them knew the truth yet. We told them what had happened. Turned up the TV. We all crammed into Zack's room. Standing. Sitting. Silent.

No one had words. Just stares and shallow breath.

Magnus came in soon after. For all his volatility, he was strangely composed. We stepped aside to talk quietly. Not about work. Not about clients. Just about keeping the staff safe. That became the only priority. *How do we protect our people?*

I called Ronni.

She was teaching in Queens and hadn't heard anything yet. I started telling her what was going on, but I could barely get the words out. My hands were shaking. I was crying without realizing it.

As we stayed on the phone, I heard her running through the school hallways. Heard her bursting into the main office. Heard the secretary reacting. The principal making an announcement. It was all happening in real time, two different worlds crashing into each other over the sound of a cell phone.

She didn't want me to hang up.

I didn't want to hang up either.

But I told her I had to stay focused and check on everyone at Emerald. I promised I'd call back when I knew more.

The phones jammed not long after. Cell towers couldn't keep up. Landlines were useless. We were cut off.

Back in Zack's room, the office was filling up.

The TV was still on. The news anchors were breathless, fumbling. Live footage showed the towers burning—black smoke pouring out of both.

Then it happened.

The first tower collapsed, right there on the screen.

No countdown. No warning. Just a shift—like the building exhaled and caved in on itself. A plume of dust erupted, racing down the streets. The camera struggled to keep up. The city folded inward.

Gasps. Hands over mouths. Someone started sobbing. Others just stood there, frozen. We watched it together, in that narrow FX suite, like we were inside a dream.

I needed air. Space. Anything that wasn't a television screen.

A few of us made our way up to the roof.

It was quiet up there.

The kind of quiet that only happens when everyone is thinking the same thing but no one knows how to say it.

We looked south. Where the towers used to be. Now there was only one. And the smoke. A giant bruise in the sky, smearing itself across the horizon.

I loved the view from our office on normal days—Empire State uptown, Twin Towers downtown. That morning, it felt like the view had betrayed us.

I didn't stay long. I couldn't. I've never done well with heights, and the rooftop was swaying in my mind. I couldn't breathe up there.

I went back down.

When I returned to Zack's room, the images had changed.

Now it was the people.

They were jumping.

Leaping from the second tower, one by one.

From that distance, on the TV, they didn't fall—they floated. Like paper dolls cut from a string. Some solo. Some in pairs. Some with arms outstretched like they were still reaching for something. Others just dropped like stones. The newscasters tried to look away, but the camera held.

Every jumper took something from us.

That's what trauma is. It's theft. Slow, quiet theft. A piece of you ripped away while you're still trying to breathe.

Then the second tower fell.

We watched it go. Sagging first. Then collapsing straight down into itself. A second cloud of dust, even thicker than the first, swallowed everything it touched.

The anchors went silent.

So were we.

No one knew what to do. We were a room full of people who made TV for a living, and we had just watched the worst thing we'd ever seen—on TV.

We didn't move. We just sat in the glow of the screen and tried not to fall apart.

I couldn't take it anymore.

The towers were gone. The jumpers had stopped falling—at least on TV—but they were still there in my mind. Floating. Twisting. Landing in the quiet.

I had to move.

I told Magnus I needed to see what was going on outside. He nodded. He got it. There wasn't much to say anymore.

When I stepped onto 22nd and headed toward 6th, the world had changed. The sidewalks were full of people, but no one was talking. Just walking. Staring. Looking downtown, where smoke now blotted out everything.

From 6th Avenue, we had a clear view south. Or we used to. Now there was just a cloud—thick and gray and endless. It swallowed the streets, the skyline, the people inside it. You couldn't tell where the city ended and the sky began.

And then I saw them.

The survivors.

Hundreds of people walking north from the Financial District. Covered in soot and dust. Eyes red. Faces streaked with tears. Some barefoot. Some dragging briefcases or purses or nothing at all. Just moving like their bodies were still running from what their minds couldn't yet process.

They looked like ghosts.

People from the neighborhood were coming out of their shops, their buildings, offering water, towels, folding chairs. One woman was handing out shoes.

There was a cash machine on the corner. I don't know why, but I walked over and took out $500. Maybe I thought if the world was ending, cash would still matter. Maybe I just needed something to feel in control of.

That's when my phone rang.

A miracle, really, that the call even got through.

It was Bobby.

He still worked at Damarc, in Midtown. He said a bunch of them were trying to get to the tunnel before it closed. They had a car. He told me if I could get there in time, they'd wait.

I didn't hesitate.

I ran back to the office, told Magnus I had a way out. By then, we'd already started helping staff figure out how to get home—those who could leave. Not everyone had a place to go. Not everyone could move yet. We didn't push. We just kept the doors open and tried to keep people feeling safe.

When it was clear that only a handful of us were left, Magnus looked at me and said, "Go. We'll figure it out tomorrow."

Tomorrow.

The word sounded fake coming out of his mouth. Like a punchline to a joke no one wanted to hear.

But I nodded, grabbed my bag, and headed out.

I started jogging toward the tunnel.

The streets were surreal—no honking, no cabs, no vendors shouting. Just people, and silence, and smoke. A city paused midsentence.

The weather was perfect, which made everything worse. A cloudless sky. Warm sun. The kind of September day that usually made you feel like the world might actually be all right. But not today. Today, it felt like the sky didn't care.

Then out of nowhere, a fighter jet screamed overhead.

The sound split the air like a blade. My body reacted before my brain could. I dropped down, pressed myself flat against the side of a building, arms over my head like I was bracing for a bomb. I didn't know if it was ours. No one did.

For a moment, I couldn't move.

I was paralyzed—not from fear, exactly, but from the unknown. From the sudden realization that *anything could happen next*.

I kept going, this time sticking closer to the buildings. Another jet passed overhead. I flinched again.

I realized I was wearing loafers—fancy ones—for a client meeting that wasn't going to happen. I never wore anything but sneakers. My feet started to ache, but I didn't stop. Somewhere in the fog of it all, I wondered if the client was still expecting me. That's how deep the conditioning ran. The city was under attack, and I was worried about missing a meeting.

I reached the tunnel and found Bobby and the others outside the car.

Eight of us piled into a tiny four-door like it was a lifeboat. Legs tangled, bags on laps, elbows in ribs—but nobody cared. We were moving. That was enough.

The ride was a blur of half-sentences and nervous laughter. We were all talking at once. Not about anything specific—just noise, because silence felt too dangerous.

We crossed into Queens. The city behind us, still burning. Still broken.

Ronni was already home. So was Bobby's girlfriend. We met at the diner on the main strip, the one dressed like the '50s—jukebox, red vinyl booths, pictures of Elvis and Little Richard on the walls.

It was packed. Everyone watching the TVs.

But Bobby and me—*we'd just come from there*. We weren't watching the horror. We were *carrying it*.

We sat down and tried to eat, but in our minds everything tasted like dust. The coffee was bitter, but I drank it anyway. I didn't know what else to do.

I was grateful to be alive. Grateful Ronni was safe. Grateful for Bobby and the others.

But I couldn't stop seeing it.

The people walking through the smoke. The paper dolls falling from the sky. The skyline collapsing like it was being erased.

I don't remember much about the next few days.

The city felt hollowed out.

Nobody smiled. Nobody honked. Nobody even made eye contact.

It was like we were all walking underwater.

I almost forgot—my brother was supposed to get married that Sunday.

Five days after the world cracked open.

Nobody knew what the hell to do.

Cancel? Postpone? Pretend the world wasn't on fire?

In the end, they kept it.

Because love didn't cancel.

Because grief was already in every corner of our lives—we might as well let some hope in, too.

The ceremony was held in a huge room lined with floor-to-ceiling windows looking out over the bay.

And right there, just beyond the glass, was a giant American flag, framed against the bruised September sky.

The water.

The sky.

The flag.

The faces of family and friends—exhausted, shell-shocked, but still standing.

For a few hours, we forgot where we were. For a few hours, we forgot what we'd lost. For a few hours, it felt like maybe—just maybe—the world wasn't completely broken.

And then Monday came.

And the world kept on bleeding.

But at least we had that day.

At least we had each other.

In the weeks that followed, I flinched at every sound.

I pressed myself into subway columns, braced for explosions that never came. I watched the skies like they were plotting something. Every low-flying plane sent my stomach to the floor. Every rumble of a train turned me to stone.

Even years later—commuting on the LIRR, standing on elevated platforms—I'd find the nearest concrete pillar and back up against it. Like if something happened, at least I'd be harder to hit.

I never talked about it much. Not really. I didn't want to. I just held on to it. Gave it a drawer like you would for a girlfriend who slept over a lot.

The world shifted that day. You didn't have to be at Ground Zero. You didn't have to know anyone who died. A piece of all of us died that day. Especially if you were there—close enough to feel it, to breathe it in.

Every September 11, the memory rises like smoke. And sometimes, without warning, I cry. Not the kind of crying you can see coming. The kind that sneaks up from behind and punches you in the ribs.

Because that day took something.

It didn't just destroy buildings. It stole the idea that we were safe. That the ground under our feet would always be there. That there would always be a tomorrow.

And I'm still trying to make peace with that.

Two months into my new job, and the hardest climb of my career got steeper. The trauma wasn't just from the attack. It was from holding space for other people's fear, from trying to lead in the middle of madness.

That day changed everything.

And not all of it came back.

**P.S.**

As I was writing this, I started to cry. Not right away. It crept in slowly, somewhere between the memories and the silence. It's been over two decades, and I thought time would dull the edges. It hasn't. Some days, the past is louder than the present.

# The Return to Section 414

While I was engaged, this older, grumpy guy I worked with gave me a piece of unsolicited advice. He made it sound like he had been married since the dawn of man. He was constantly complaining about his wife. Like, he wouldn't shut up about it. I kept thinking, *Dude, first of all, you're no picnic—and if you're so damn unhappy, why are you still married to her?* Maybe he just had nothing better to talk about. Honestly, I'm sure his wife was probably an angel, considering what a sad sack he was.

He was an engineer, so definitely a particular breed. Old, tacky T-shirts with dumb sayings like THIS IS MY I HATE MY JOB SHIRT or DON'T TALK TO ME. I'M BUSY. He always wore jeans that were two sizes too big, so his ass crack made regular guest appearances whenever he knelt down to fix equipment. I never understood why his pants were massive but his shirts fit like Saran Wrap. And yet, as curmudgeonly as he was, he was really funny. He'd say all kinds of wild shit. Sometimes I wasn't even sure if he was talking to me or just narrating the movie in his head, but I didn't care—I got a kick out of it.

Anyway, the advice was simple: *Before you get married, commit to something regular—bowling, softball, poker night—anything that gives you a built-in excuse to get out of the house. But you have to do it before the wedding, so she can't tell you no.*

I nodded and laughed. But I hated bowling, wasn't about to join a book club, and didn't really have anything like that lined up. Plus, I was already living with my wife-to-be, so unless I pretended I'd been sneaking out weekly without her noticing, it was gonna be hard to sell.

But then I had a revelation.

What could I do that involved drinking, that happened regularly, and that no one would think twice about?

Holy shit. Perfect.

Hockey.

I had plenty of friends who would go to Rangers games. We all worked in the city and commuted through Penn Station—right beneath Madison Square Garden. Ronni already knew how obsessed I was. She had lived through the Rangers' '94 Cup run with me. This would be a completely normal evolution. If the other guys got permission from their partners, she'd have no choice.

She wasn't dumb. She knew they sold alcohol at the Garden. If the amount I drank watching games on TV was any clue, she had no illusions that it would be one beer and a hot dog. But she trusted me. For now.

So I hit up a few friends to test the waters. My brother was in. A couple of college buddies. Even a dude from work who wasn't a Rangers fan, but he was Canadian—so, yeah, hockey. I also called Ray. We always bonded over the Rangers. Total no-brainer.

Everyone in that group drank, so I knew there would be pre-game drinks and in-game drinks. Ray was a bit more like me, though. He drank heavy. Maybe too heavy. And he had a thing for pills, especially Percocet. Always had a bag of them like they were Skittles.

We bought a half-season: twenty games. Three a month, give or take. If the team made the playoffs, it could stretch another two months of scheduled and perfectly legitimate drinking.

None of us had much money, so the expensive seats were out. But I didn't care. I immediately checked Section 414—the blue seats— where my friend Stephanie had sat all those years ago. That's where it all started for me. It felt symbolic. Perfect, even. But 414 wasn't available. So we grabbed Section 417—close enough. Just a few short steps from my old stomping ground.

This was going to be perfect.

And it was. That turned into a twelve-year run with season tickets. Guys rotated in and out, but Ray and I were the constants. It was exactly what I expected. We'd meet at Charley O's in Penn Station before the game, usually around 6 p.m. for a 7 p.m. puck drop. It was an event every time. Season tickets weren't just a fun hobby—they were an identity. People treated you like a VIP. Clients wanted to go, friends would ask if you had extras. When I owned my own company, I even persuaded my business partner to let the company foot the bill.

We had a ritual. Pre-game: two or three beers. Sometimes a shot. First period: two pints of the worst, most expensive beer imaginable. Between periods: two more beers and a hot dog and knish. At that point we were six or seven drinks deep, and then came the Percocets.

Ray and I were the only ones taking them. He had legit back issues and had undergone spinal fusion surgery. That's what got him hooked. Convenient for me, maybe even a blessing in disguise. He didn't just take one—he chewed them. He was always stoned. And I think he liked that I took pills, too. There's something about shared secrecy that bonds people. Drinking and smoking was socially acceptable. Pills were different. We didn't advertise it. We didn't share.

I usually stuck to one or two pills. For me, it was still all about the drinking. Sports and alcohol were like peanut butter and jelly. Pure joy.

By the third period, they stopped serving alcohol, so we had to act fast. For a while, that meant two more beers each—bringing the night's total to eight or nine. But eventually, that wasn't enough. So I started sneaking off for two vodka Red Bulls.

Yeah, I know. Not pretty.

Eight or nine beers. Two vodka Red Bulls. One or two Percs. Maybe a hit of weed. If I went to two hundred games during those years, I probably remember five. By the second period, I was seeing double. Could barely walk.

The Percs always fucked me. I knew they would. And I took them anyway.

My brain wasn't wired for moderation. Not with alcohol. Not with pills. Not with anything.

There were nights I'd sneak off into the men's room just to puke my guts out so I could come back and drink more. That was normal. Just a detour. Nothing out of the ordinary.

Puking and blacking out were staples in my game-night routine.

If I had to take a dump on the ice and thought I could get away with it, I probably would have.

That's where I was.

And the thing is—being there felt weirdly right.

There was something about being back in that building, up in those blue seats, that made me feel like I was home again. Like I was twelve years old, sitting next to Stephanie, hearing the crowd explode, high on belonging and sugar and sound.

But the truth is, that was also where I had my first real exposure to drinking and drugging. Not just the act of it—but the feeling that it was normal. That it belonged there. That it belonged with me.

It's no wonder I found my way back. Of course I did. It felt like going back to the place where the blueprint was drawn. The problem was, the return trip was darker, messier, and lonelier than I ever imagined it could be.

Now, when I'm at a game with my kid or a sober friend, I look around and wonder, *How the hell did I survive this?*

Getting home was its own game. If I caught a train, staying awake long enough to get off at the right stop was a small miracle. One time, someone stole my hat right off my head, and I woke up in Babylon—the last stop on the line—with a conductor shaking me to make sure I was still breathing.

But the part that haunts me the most?

Driving home from the train station.

When we lived in the apartment, I took the subway and walked. That was at least safer—for everyone else. But after we bought the house, I had to drive four or five miles home. Blackout drunk. Stumbling into my car. Barely functional.

I'd lock my eyes on the yellow line in the middle of the road like it was a lifeline. Windows open. Radio blasting. Slapping my face. Talking out loud:

"You can do this. Just get home. You can do this."

I never crashed. Never got pulled over. Never killed anyone.

But not because I wasn't asking for it.

A wife. Two kids. And I was out here running a deathwish three times a month.

You hear stories—families torn apart by a drunk driver. Kids dead. Parents shattered. Futures gone.

And I was one blackout away from being that story.

What a stupid, selfish fuck I was.

I'm not sure this is what the engineer had in mind when he gave me that little bit of advice. But it almost killed me.

# Sudden Death

After camp, Ray and I stayed close. We had some wild times visiting each other in college—partying, drinking, smoking, doing lines. The kind of chaos that felt like freedom at the time. We didn't talk much about anything serious. We were just living fast, numbing whatever pain we were carrying.

Then we lost touch for a few years. No falling out, just life happening. Work, relationships, survival in general. And then, in 1994, during the Rangers' legendary Cup run, I ran into Ray at Madison Square Garden. Of all places. It was like fate reached out, smacked us on the back of the head, and said, "Get back to it."

Turns out, we had both moved to Queens. We were practically neighbors. It didn't take long before we were best friends all over again. We got season tickets to the Rangers. We went on a dozen camping trips. He was in my wedding party. My wife loved him. Everyone loved him. He was still the same magnetic, hilarious, bigger-than-life guy I met at sleepaway camp. And just like back then, he was still running hot—drinking, partying, pushing limits. But so was I.

Hockey became our thing. Ritual. Identity. Escape. If we weren't watching the game, we were talking about the game. The Garden was our church. And then life threw another curveball.

Ray got sick.

At first, they thought it was manageable. The cancer was in his stomach. The doctors were optimistic. With treatment, they could shrink the tumors. Maybe even beat it. But that didn't happen. It only got worse. It spread. Liver. Lungs. Eventually, his brain.

He didn't tell a lot of people right away. That wasn't Ray's style. He kept it quiet. And he never, ever complained. Even as he lost weight. Even when the pain got unbearable. He'd crack jokes. Shrug it off. He didn't want pity.

About six months into his illness, I had an idea. Opening night at Madison Square Garden was coming up, and I knew how much it meant to both of us. He wasn't sure he'd be able to go. He felt like shit. But I told him I'd keep the ticket open for him until the very last second.

"If you feel up to it," I said, "call me. I'll be waiting."

The night before the game, I wrote an email to Adam Graves. *The* Adam Graves. One of the greatest Rangers of all time. I figured it was a shot in the dark, but I wanted Ray to know how much that night meant. I wanted to give him something bigger than the game.

The next morning, my phone rang. It was Adam Graves. Calling me. He told me he'd set aside a private skybox and would come by during the game to bring us up to watch a period with him. Just the three of us.

That night, Ray made it out. Barely. But he made it. The Rangers won 5–2. We watched a period with Adam Graves. We laughed. We cried. I watched Ray light up in a way I hadn't seen in months. It was magic.

He never forgot that night. Neither did I.

I was still drinking when he got diagnosed that summer. That night with Adam Graves—that was October 2009. He had already started to fade, but he showed up. I got sober five months later, in March 2010. And thank God I did. Because if I hadn't, I never would've survived what came next. I never would've been able to show up for him—not fully. Not like I did.

As the months went on, things got worse. He needed an eyepatch. Brain surgery left a scar like someone tried to carve the pain out of his head. He could barely talk. He was down to 110 pounds. Still—he never complained. He'd roll around in a wheelchair with a tray of pills, yelling, "Cigars! Cigarettes!" like he was working a comedy club in the Catskills. He was dying. But he was still Ray.

Near the end, I helped organize a fundraiser for him. He showed up in a wheelchair, eyepatch, scar, the whole nine. He looked like he had one foot in the next life already. But he showed up. We raised $40,000 that day. Everyone from camp came. Saul and Helen came too—the first time I'd seen them since the day I stormed out of camp.

I hugged them like my life depended on it. I told them I was sorry. That I regretted every second of leaving. That they always meant the world to me. I told them I got sober. Saul nodded. Helen cried. She told me they were proud of me. That they were sorry it caused me so much pain. That moment took a boulder off my chest. Helen still writes me when she reads something I post. She never stopped being a camp mom.

We also threw a reunion for Ray. He didn't want it—said it was too much trouble. But we knew. We all knew. It was his living funeral. The last time we'd all be together.

In 2014, the Rangers made another incredible run to the Stanley Cup Finals. I watched almost every playoff game with Ray—at his apartment or in the hospital. Matt joined us whenever he could. Ray was fading fast by then, but I think a part of him was holding on, just in case they pulled it off. I was hoping, too. They almost did. But they got slaughtered in the Finals. A month later, Ray died.

Toward the end, I got to hold his hand. I told him I loved him. That I'd never forget him. He told me to look after his wife and five year old son. Watching him fade in front of his kid was almost too much to bear.

I never cried while he was sick. Not once. I stayed strong. Maybe too strong. But at the funeral, I cracked. I walked to the grave with Matt beside me, shovel in hand. I dropped dirt on the casket and broke open. Years of pain, grief, shame—everything came pouring out. I sobbed. Snot. Shaking. Matt held me like a brother.

And then Ray's wife came over, hugged me tight, and whispered, "If Ray is watching, he's probably calling you a big pussy."

I laughed through the tears. Because of course he would.

Matt died eight or nine years later. Cancer again. Faster. Just as brutal. The three of us had once been invincible. Now it's just me. I should've been the one to go. I lived like I wanted to die. And yet here I am.

Maybe I have survivor's guilt. I miss them every day. I think about the camping trips, the hockey games, the nights we made each other laugh until we couldn't breathe. Ray never got sober. He never stopped numbing. I don't know if it would've made a difference. But I wish we had talked more about the important stuff.

We were the same sickness in different bodies. Mirrors.

He never made it out.

But because of him, I did.

# The First Drink Gets You Drunk

B efore Ronni and I had kids, it felt like there wasn't much at stake. My drinking didn't really have consequences because it was just us. Most of the time I'd stumble in late from work or some event, crawl into bed, and pass out. No kids to wake up, no one to take care of. By that time, Ronni knew I drank too much. But I usually managed not to make a complete fool of myself in social situations. Not to say I didn't act like an idiot from time to time—but nothing I couldn't talk my way out of. There were signs. But I made them seem normal. I justified everything.

When we lived in an apartment, we always had alcohol in the house. And weed. Always way too much alcohol, like I was a doomsday prepper. At first, it was just a case of Budweiser in the fridge. Maybe a bottle of vodka. A couple bottles of wine "in case" we had company. Then it became more curated. We'd go out for sushi and I'd have a Sapporo. The next day, a case of Sapporo would be in the fridge. Same with Blue Moon, with the obligatory orange slice. Foster's oil cans on the train ride home? I started stocking those, too. Guinness? Tried it, but it tasted like sun-cooked coffee grounds.

When we moved into our house, I convinced Ronni to buy a wine rack—because it was "furniture," not because I needed the wine. Trips to the liquor store felt like Black Friday. I'd come home with bottles of red, white, Prosecco (for Ronni), Veuve Clicquot in case we celebrated something, gin (Tanqueray, for Grandpa), vodka, whiskey, rum, tequila, even blackberry brandy for nostalgia. This wasn't occasional—it was every time. Our fridge looked like a Beverage Barn. Our basement like a wine cellar and the recycle bin like a dumpster in the back of a bar. Just like the Super Balls, the Smurfs, the hockey cards—nothing in moderation. Ever.

Ronni would ask why we needed so much and how expensive it all was. But somehow, I always got a pass. We entertained more than our friends, so I needed to be prepared. At one point, my stepmom, Dominique, worked for a French travel agency and got heavy discounts on alcohol. She'd ask if I wanted anything. I told her I bought in bulk to gift to clients during the holidays. It sounded legit. She believed it—or at least pretended to. I'd order cases of Grey Goose and Absolut. When they arrived, I'd drive to her office, load the boxes into my car, bring them home, and arrange them neatly in a basement closet. Twenty-four bottles of vodka stacked like treasure. I never gave a single one away. I brought a few to work and stashed them under my desk. I drank out with friends, clients, coworkers. But my favorite was drinking alone at home.

After work, I'd pour a vodka and Diet Coke in one of those massive thirty-two-ounce plastic cups. Three-quarters vodka, splash of Diet Coke, some ice. One drink—technically. But really? More like five or six. I could always say, "I only had one." And I meant it—sort of. "One" just meant different things to different people.

On nights we went out, I'd pre-game. One or two before dinner, maybe more. Sometimes Ronni knew. Sometimes she didn't. If I pulled it off, I'd ask, "Mind if I have one before dinner?" Already half in the bag. I had it down.

My pill habit never took center stage. Ronni never knew about it. I always hid it. When I couldn't get painkillers, I'd pivot—Benadryl and NyQuil. Two Benadryl and a shot of NyQuil hit like a Percocet. If Ronni asked, I'd say it was allergies or a cold. Cough syrup with codeine? Heaven.

My father-in-law was in a near-fatal car wreck once. He was prescribed pain meds, but he wasn't a fan of taking them. So they just sat there in the guest bathroom. I homed in on them like a drug-sniffing dog at the border. I stole a few at a time. Strategically. Carefully. Never enough to raise suspicion.

Ronni got migraines and was prescribed something strong. She hated taking it unless it was bedtime. Said it made her drowsy. Drowsy? Perfect. Into the stash it went.

Addicts are resourceful.

Everything got harder when we had kids. We were exhausted. We both worked. We had two little humans to keep alive. Date nights were rare. Dinners out were a treat. Ronni usually drove. She didn't drink much—not her thing, and she knew I couldn't be trusted to drive after. More than once, she'd ask, "Can you just have one drink tonight so I don't have to drive?" And every time, I'd say yes. And I meant it. I truly believed I could stop at one.

But I couldn't.

Sometimes I'd sneak extras early in the night. If she didn't notice, I'd keep going. Even if I knew I wasn't safe to drive, I'd do it anyway—because getting yelled at felt worse than getting pulled over. That's how twisted my thinking was. It didn't feel like a choice. It just happened.

When she did notice, she'd ask, "I thought you said just one drink?" She was rightfully angry. And somehow, I'd still turn it around. Make it her fault. Like she had no right to question me. Like it didn't matter.

I was such an asshole.

It always came back to that one question: *Why can't you just have one drink?*

I never had an answer.

I'd say, "No one has just one," or "What's the difference?" or "I can handle more." But the truth? I didn't know why I couldn't stop. I never could. No one had ever asked me that until Ronni did.

If I knew the answer, maybe I could've stopped.

Blaming others was easier. Making excuses was easier. But it was exhausting. Lying. Hiding. Fighting over something so stupid— something that was always my fault.

One time stands out. A day I knew something was really wrong with me. A sign I wasn't okay. A moment I felt helpless. Fucked.

We were invited to a BBQ at our friends' house—Mick and Sasha. They lived about forty minutes away. Big party. Lots of booze. I was excited. Mick liked to drink, so I always looked forward to hanging with him. Our daughters were maybe two and six. On the drive, Ronni asked if I could not drink so she could relax and have a couple drinks herself. She rarely asked that. She deserved that. I promised.

We got there. It was summer. Hot. Kids everywhere. Probably fifty people total. Ronni was talking with friends. I walked over to the cooler and grabbed a cold Budweiser.

I couldn't resist a cold beer from a cooler on a summer day. That's like dangling a carrot in front of a donkey. I crushed it. No one noticed. Cracked another. Sipped it while talking to friends. Then another. Still early. I'd sober up in time. No harm, right?

A few beers later, I was sitting with Mick, already buzzing. Ronni walked over with our daughters and a bunch of other kids. I had a beer in hand. I tried to act sober.

She asked if I'd been drinking. I said no—just the one. She gave me a wad of cash. "The ice cream truck's here. Can you take the kids?"

She stared at me. Stern. Testing. Maybe hoping I'd prove her wrong.

I stood up. Wobbled.

I looked at Mick like a kid caught with his dad's *Playboy*. The kids were staring, ready to move. I was the Pied Piper of poor decisions.

We walked toward the front lawn. Their house sat on a slight incline. My legs were Jello. I heard the ice cream truck. The kids ran. I followed. Kinda. My daughters were yelling for me to hurry.

I got to the top of the lawn and leaned on the truck. The driver asked what we wanted. I couldn't speak. Couldn't focus. Couldn't count the money in my hand. The kids were shouting their orders. I handed the guy the cash and hoped for the best.

Then I stumbled. Backward. Lost balance. Rolled down the lawn like a drunk bowling ball.

I was done.

Lying there. Wasted. In the grass. In front of my kids. In front of everyone. Like a real drunk. Not a joke. Not the funny guy. Just pathetic.

I don't remember much after that.

I was in the passenger seat, slurring, while Ronni drove home. The kids were asleep in the back after what should've been a perfect day.

Except for me.

Why couldn't I have just one drink?

Why?

What the hell was wrong with me?

Ronni was furious. I couldn't blame her. I didn't even have an excuse anymore. Not one that made sense.

Years later, in a meeting, someone said, "The first drink always gets you drunk."

I didn't get it at first. The math didn't add up.

But eventually, it did.

That was the answer. The one I never had when Ronni asked. Why couldn't I have just one drink?

Because I couldn't. Not then. Not ever.

One always meant two. Which meant five. Which meant ten.

The first drink always got me drunk.

Every single time.

# The Weight

When our daughters were about two and six, work was still everything.

It consumed me.

There was nothing left over.

I had been at Emerald Cut for seven years.

Business was booming.

And I was disappearing.

Life had become an endless parade of tasks, crises, deadlines.

A slow bleed of identity.

The clients.

The jobs.

The fires Magnus would start and then demand I put out.

If business slowed down even a little,

the dread would settle into my gut like wet cement.

Not just fear for myself—

but fear for the whole company.

For the employees.

For their families.

For their mortgages and grocery bills.

My name wasn't at the top of the paperwork.

I wasn't the majority owner.

But I might as well have been.

I carried it all.

Magnus had invested more over the years,

and he owned most of the company.

He shouldered the financial burden on paper.

But emotionally,

he handed most of it to me.

He made sure I knew how important I was—

how *indispensable*—

but deep down,

I always knew whose company it really was.

I still craved the credit.

The status.

The illusion of being an owner.

I loved it when people thought I was more important than I was.

I needed it.

When things went well, he took the bows.

When things went wrong, I threw myself between the blowback and everyone else.

When money got tight,

Magnus and I both cut our salaries to save jobs.

We made the same sacrifices.

Even if we didn't carry the same weight.

Ronni hated it.

She hated that I took the same hit when he had so much more to lose.

But I always brushed it off:

*That's just the way it is.*

Because the truth was,

explaining it—

admitting how unfair it felt—

meant I'd have to *feel* it.

And feeling anything was too dangerous back then.

The company grew like I'd dreamed it would.

But so did the pressure.

More clients.

More jobs.

More people.

More dinners, events, pitches, flights, smiles.

I lived and breathed Emerald.

It was my oxygen.

And it was slowly killing me.

Inside, I was a landfill.

Grief, rage, sadness—

all buried under the surface,

compacted so tight I didn't even recognize it anymore.

I had tried therapy.

But I wasn't capable of being honest yet.

Not with a stranger.

Not with Ronni.

Not with myself.

I couldn't even find the words.

All I knew was that I was exhausted.

Empty.

Crumbling under the weight of being "the strong one."

I loved my family.

I loved my girls with a desperation that sometimes scared me.

I would have thrown myself in front of a train for them without
hesitation.

But there were nights I sat in my car,

hands clenched on the steering wheel,

and wished I didn't have to walk through the front door.

Wished I could just keep driving.

Disappear.

Not because I didn't love them.

But because I didn't feel like I deserved them.

On the outside, everything looked perfect.

Beautiful wife.

Adorable kids.

House.

Cars.

Vacations.

Always something new and shiny.

And I hated that I couldn't enjoy any of it.

It wasn't constant misery.

There were real moments of joy—

tickle fights on the floor,

Saturday morning pancakes,

little arms wrapped around my neck.

But underneath it all was the whisper:

*You don't belong here.*

*You don't deserve this.*

*It's only a matter of time before they figure it out.*

That voice had been with me since I was a kid.

And it wasn't going anywhere.

The drinking was constant.

Maybe not a daily blackout,

but a daily negotiation.

Vodka under the desk to take the edge off the end of the day.

Two beers on the train home.

Maybe a painkiller.

Maybe another drink before dinner.

Just enough to dull it.

Just enough to keep the tightrope from snapping.

If I wasn't numbing,

I was simmering.

Always ready to boil over.

Always afraid I would.

I know now—working in behavioral health—

that this was textbook burnout.

Textbook untreated depression.

Textbook self-destruction.

But back then,

all I knew was that I had one weapon left:

**numbness.**

I couldn't manufacture happiness.

But I could sit in sadness.

Settle into it like a coffin.

Smile through it.

Pretend it wasn't eating me alive.

At home, I was never cruel.

Never violent.

Never dangerous.

But I stole something more subtle from my family—

something harder to see:

Safety.

Warmth.

Emotional security.

Ronni was always willing to listen.

To help.

But I wouldn't let her in.

The fear of being known was worse than the pain of staying hidden.

Most nights, I'd mumble about stress, climb into bed, and disappear.

Even when I was awake,

I wasn't really there.

Our oldest daughter started developing tics.

Eyebrow picking.

Wrist rolling.

Endless blinking.

We took her to doctors.

Specialists.

Everyone said she was fine.

But she wasn't fine.

She was feeling the weather inside our house—

the pressure system I had created without even realizing it.

Children are barometers.

They know when the air shifts.

They know when it's not safe to relax.

I thought I was protecting them.

I thought I was hiding it well enough.

But kids don't listen to what you say.

They listen to what you are.

And what I was—

without ever meaning to be—

was absent.

Then came the fall of 2008.

The banks collapsed.

The economy crumbled.

The floor we had been tap-dancing on vanished.

Magnus and I huddled together like survivors after a storm.

We called an emergency staff meeting.

Told them there would be pay cuts.

Maybe 10 percent, maybe 20 percent.

Maybe more.

We promised we'd do everything we could to protect them.

But we knew the truth:

We had no idea what was coming.

None of us did.

But after 9/11, we believed we could survive anything.

We'd already lived through the unthinkable.

Everything after that?

It felt like turbulence.

But behind closed doors, Magnus and I were panicking. Whispering worst-case scenarios like bedtime stories.

And then...

It passed.

Not the world's suffering—ours.

Somehow, we came out unscathed.

Within months, we had bounced back. Hard.

The work came pouring in. We rolled back the pay cuts.

It felt like we'd beaten the system. Like we were untouchable.

We expanded to a second floor. Opened a new division. Hired more people.

And in the middle of it all, while the paint was still drying, I pitched Magnus on a beer tap for the kitchen.

Told him it would boost morale. That the team had earned it. That the clients would love it.

And they did.

But that wasn't why I wanted it.

The truth was simple and pathetic and dangerous:

I needed it.

A beer tap in the office.

An IV drip disguised as a perk.

One more way to blur the line between coping and celebration.

We told ourselves we were building something.

But what I was building—very quietly, very efficiently—was a cage.

One drink at a time.

# Part Three
# I'm Better

# Confessions of a Daddy Blogger

While I was drowning in work, Grey Goose, and diapers—naturally, I started a parenting blog.

I needed an outlet. Even though I was technically in the "creative" business, there was nothing inspiring about editing commercials for psoriasis cream and extra-strength maxi pads. That didn't fill my creative bucket. It barely filled a thimble.

I'd always considered myself a writer, but I hadn't touched that part of myself in years. Too much pressure. Too much noise. Too many hangovers. But then I stumbled into the world of parenting blogs. Mostly moms. Some were heartfelt, some were hilarious, and all of them were drowning in wine references. There were dad blogs, too, but they either felt too vanilla or tried way too hard to be edgy. None of them sounded like me.

So I started one.

Ronni and I were in the thick of it—two daughters, six and two. Total opposites. Hilarious little weirdos. Parenting was surreal. The giving birth part. The hospital. Naming a human. It felt like something out of a movie. But nobody tells you what comes after the credits—the sleep deprivation, formula runs, the kind of screaming that melts brain cells. Once we got through the gauntlet, the fun started to creep in. The weird stuff. The funny stuff. The stuff that makes you feel like you're losing your mind but also like you're part of something miraculous.

I loved spending time with them. For a few minutes at a time, they made me feel whole. Like maybe I had a purpose. They were the only people in my life who didn't know I was broken. They thought I was perfect. And I loved that.

There were moments when I thought, *Maybe this is it. Maybe they'll be the thing that saves me.* But the emptiness always came back—stronger, deeper, darker. My kids couldn't fix my depression, my anxiety, or my drinking. In some ways, having kids made it worse. More pressure. More responsibility. More things I could screw up.

I had to be "on" all the time. At work, at home, even in my own damn head. So I drank more. Smoked more. Popped more pills. Kept my sippy cup full. My kids even started asking if I had "Daddy juice" in my glass before they took a sip. It was funny... until it wasn't.

But something about being around them cracked something open in me. Their honesty. Their chaos. Their purity. I started writing again. Just little things at first—jotting down the wacked out shit they said. The beautiful moments. The total disasters. And for the first time in a long time, I felt like I had a voice again.

I launched the blog within days. Classic addict move: find a thing, obsess over it, build a brand before the coffee gets cold. I called it *Out-Numbered*. I think Ronni came up with the name. I was the only guy in a house full of girls. Get it?

I wrote constantly. At work, at home, on the train. I posted three or four times a week. The posts were funny, raw, and brutally honest. No Pinterest crafts. No airbrushed perfection. Just the real stuff.

Imperfect parenting from a dad who was trying—and sometimes failing—to keep it together.

People noticed. First friends. Then strangers. Then the mom bloggers. They shared my stuff, hyped me up, and brought me into their world. I became the token dad at the mommy blog party. Good dads are sexy to moms, right? Especially girl dads.

The validation hit like a drug. Comments. Shares. Likes. I checked them like a lunatic. I was getting an insane amount of views every month. Parenting sites were calling me one of the top dad bloggers in the space. A pop culture magazine gave me a column.

*Working Mother* magazine named me one of the "25 Dads Who Rock." The list included celebrity dads like Brad Pitt, Will Smith, Barack Obama... and me. Yeah, the fucking president. My wife thought it was a joke. It wasn't.

And then there was the Mommy Blogger Convention.

Three thousand moms. Maybe twenty dads. I was the only dad presenting. I walked on stage, paused, looked out at the sea of women, and said:

"My penis is so confused right now."

They lost it.

I read a Valentine's Day post I'd written—funny, self-deprecating, unexpectedly sweet. It landed. The crowd laughed, clapped. But I remember walking off stage feeling like I had gotten away with something. Like I was living two lives—and this one, the public one, was the lie.

Nobody knew that my drinking was out of control. Or that I was struggling with crippling depression. Or that every comment and click was just another fix.

I even wrote a breakup letter to beer once. I called it "It's Not You, It's Me."

*I just wanted to let you know that I really appreciate all you have done for me and how accessible you have been over the past twenty years or so. I know this sounds corny but you've been a real friend to me... but I've found someone else. Her name is Vodka.*

Funny at the time.

Now? Just sad.

The blog became my identity. I wasn't just a dad. I was the dad blogger. The funny one. The raw one. The one who "told it like it is." But I wasn't telling it like it really was. Not the whole thing.

I never wrote about the time I almost fell down the stairs drunk while holding my two-year-old.

Or about how Ronni and I were barely speaking by the end.

How the tension in the house was thick enough to choke on.

I never wrote about driving drunk or not coming home some nights, too shit-faced to get on the train.

Instead, I posted about New Year's resolutions and mantras like they were going to save me. One year, I even got a tattoo on my arm that said STRENGTH. TRUTH. LOVE. I wasn't drunk when I got it. I was just desperate. I thought if I carved the words into my skin, maybe they'd sink into my soul.

They didn't.

I wrote a post that night and signed off with:

*All I need to do this year is look in the mirror. It's not a lot to ask of oneself. Just be better.*

But I wasn't getting better.

And it was too painful to look in the mirror.

I was performing.

Everything I wrote was filtered through a fog of addiction, shame, and the constant need to be seen.

And then, right at the end—three days before I got sober—I wrote about taking my daughter to the circus.

A full-circle moment.

A flash of real connection.

I compared her cotton-candy kisses to the ones my mom used to give me.

That one still gets me.

In the end, I'm glad I have those posts to look back on. A messy, chaotic, sometimes hilarious journal of a time in my life that was anything but perfect—not even close—but still captured moments I never want to forget.

It's also a love letter to my kids. A record of what it felt like to be their dad during those early years. Even if I didn't always get it right.

The good. The bad. The absurd.

They're all there.

And so was I.

# Dead Man Commuting

At first, the commute into the city wasn't bad.

Less than an hour each way—just enough time to read, doze, stare out the window, and feel like part of something bigger.

Work gave me purpose then.

Something to focus on.

Something to chase.

Something that made me feel like I was worth a damn.

Commuting was just part of the deal—

an occupational hazard.

A rite of passage.

In the beginning, I didn't mind it.

I took it all in like a wide-eyed tourist:

the working masses shuffling through Penn Station like cattle;

the middle-aged men playing poker on cardboard tables;

the women painting their faces on, one eyelash at a time;

the moms herding strollers toward Central Park.

And the holy grail: the bar car.

Every night on the way home, you sprinted down the platform, hoping to squeeze through the doors of the one car that would soften the crash landing from Manhattan back to suburbia.

A bar inside a moving train.

Convenient.

Necessary.

Brilliant.

Those first few years made me feel grown up.

It felt like a win.

Like a secret handshake into adulthood.

But time passed.

Life got heavier.

More pressure.

More bills.

More responsibility.

And the commute stopped feeling like a secret handshake.

It started feeling like a chokehold.

The days got longer.

The hours bled together.

And the commute—once a badge of honor—became the period at the end of the longest, ugliest run-on sentence in the world.

I tried to sleep, but my mind wouldn't stop racing.

I tried to read, but I couldn't hold onto a single sentence for more than a second.

All I wanted was a teleportation button—

something to zap me home,

to my daughters,

before they went to sleep and I lost another day I could never get back.

The train could mean the difference between tucking them in at night

or missing them for another twenty-four hours.

The train could mean the difference between being a dad,

or being a ghost.

And then there were the people.

The noise.

The bare feet on the seats.

The half-eaten tuna melts leaking onto laps.

The endless phone calls shouted at maximum volume.

The human zoo that made you hate everyone, including yourself.

I started to come apart.

Slowly.

Quietly.

So I drank.

Two Foster's oil cans to go.

50.8 ounces of anesthesia.

Not to "take the edge off."

But to erase the whole fucking day.

At some point, the whole ride started to feel like a bad movie—

a human zoetrope,

the same sad scenes flickering past my eyes,

looping and looping until I wanted to punch my way out of the frame.

When the beer wasn't enough,

I turned to something else.

I wrote.

Tiny laptop jammed onto my knees.

Napkins, scraps of paper, receipts.

Whatever I could find.

Writing was different.

Writing made it survivable.

Observing was one thing.

Documenting was another.

If I could put it down in words,

it wasn't happening *to* me—

it was happening *around* me.

Writing made it less real.

Made it manageable.

Made it almost funny.

I wrote about the absurdity.

The sadness.

The anger.

The stupid, human moments that made me feel like I was still awake inside my own skin.

I kept train diaries.

Dozens of them.

Filed away in folders, journals, email drafts, pizza-stained napkins.

It wasn't art.

It wasn't therapy.

It was survival.

If you want to know where my head was back then,

you don't have to guess.

Just read the *Train Diaries.*

They're not just journal entries. They're confessions. Breadcrumbs dropped in blackout fog—some angry, some aching, all of them desperate to be found.

# The "If Onlys"

I spent years believing that *just one more thing* would fix me. If only I got the promotion.

If only I made six figures.

If only we moved out of that apartment.

If only we bought the house.

If only we had kids.

If only I looked better.

If only people saw me the way I wanted to be seen.

Then I'd stop.

Then I'd calm down.

Then I'd drink like a normal person.

Or maybe I wouldn't drink at all.

And for a while—*sometimes*—it worked.

A raise would let me buy things that made me feel like someone else.

A new couch. A new car. A new version of me.

Each "if only" would buy me a few weeks where I didn't hate myself in the mirror.

But the shine always wore off.

And when it did, I was still there.

Me. Same wiring. Same ghosts. Same sickness.

Turns out, the "if onlys" are just hope dressed up in a straitjacket.

They look like progress. They feel like purpose.

But they're just distractions—soft lies that whisper, *One more thing and you'll be okay.*

The only thing worse than not getting what you want

is getting it...

and realizing it doesn't fix the hole.

I chased that voice for years.

Until, one day, I ran out of "next things."

And had no choice but to look at the thing I'd been running from all along.

Me.

# Lost Car, Found Rock Bottom

Then came the night I wound up on my front lawn at 3 a.m., puking my guts out. I didn't remember how I got home. My car was nowhere to be found. I had no clue where I'd been.

I had gone out with clients to celebrate the end of a big job. Taking clients out was just part of the business culture—an easy excuse to justify drinking. To everyone else. And to myself.

The night started at Emerald. A little pregame session—beers, wine, good vibes. That's the thing: it always started out normal. I never thought, *Hey, let's get obliterated and black out tonight.* I went in thinking I'd have fun and go home.

Then we hit this amazing restaurant downtown. Fancy place. I'd always wanted to try it. We ordered everything. I remember the bone marrow appetizer. It was delicious at the time. Now, just the thought of it makes me want to hurl. We downed five or six bottles of wine, plus my usual vodka and Diet Cokes. Everyone else seemed fine. I was already seeing double.

That's the worst moment—the tipping point. When you *know* you're losing control, but you also *know* you can't stop. Once that switch flips, the brakes are gone.

After dinner, the clients wanted to keep going. Someone suggested a bar nearby. No idea where it was or if I agreed, but we ended up there anyway. The next thing I remember is being in the bathroom, wobbling at the urinal. Then... nothing. Blackout.

Meanwhile, I had told my wife I wouldn't be late. It was a weeknight. I was supposed to get the kids ready for school in the morning. I'm sure my phone was stacked with twenty missed calls from her. When I know I've fucked up, I shut down. *I'm in trouble anyway,* I tell myself, *so what's the point in answering? She'll just yell. I'll feel worse.*

I have a hazy memory of wearing someone's pashmina and punching one of my employees in the arm. There was even a picture of me floating around online—thank you, Facebook. Then I remember the bathroom floor at Penn Station. I was puking into a toilet, barely conscious. Next thing? I'm on my lawn at 3 a.m., emptying my stomach again.

At 6:30 a.m., my wife woke me up. Her face said it all—pure disgust. But this time was different. She wasn't angry. She was done. She wasn't mad. She pitied me. And that hurt worse.

She stormed out, leaving me to deal with the kids—ages seven and three. I was still drunk. Struggled to dress them, fed them God knows what, and got them out the door. One small problem: *Where the fuck is my car?*

I scanned the street, confused. My kids asking where the car was. I had no answer. Maybe it was at the train station? Maybe I took a car service and puked in the backseat? Why was I at Penn Station? None of it made sense.

It was winter. Cold. My oldest was up ahead when I saw her talking to someone in an SUV. It was my neighbor Teddy. He saw I was struggling and offered us a ride to school. Lifesaver. We all climbed in.

I'd had plenty of drinks with Teddy before. I figured I'd tell him about my night and we'd laugh it off. But before I could open my mouth, his daughter piped in from the backseat:

"You smell like alcohol."

Boom. Perspective shift. Like my brain took a hard right, blew through a stop sign, and crashed full speed into a new reality.

We got to the school. My daughter climbed out—no jacket. It was freezing. Then she turned and said, "Daddy, I don't have any lunch."

Teddy's daughter offered her an apple from her lunchbox.

I was crumbling.

Teddy drove me to the train station. My car was there. I buckled my youngest into the car seat and headed to daycare. When we got there, the daycare workers started laughing. I was confused—until they pointed out her dress was on backward.

Normally, I'd make a joke. Father of the year and all that. But not today. Today, it wasn't funny. I was mortified. I felt like a loser. I wanted to cry.

I drove home. Called into work and lied—said my daughter was sick. More lies. More shame.

I was wrecked. Not just hungover—broken. I had failed my wife and kids. This wasn't just a few blackouts anymore. This was my family taking the hits. My life was like a garbage truck flinging trash onto every car on the road behind me.

The shame was suffocating.

That day, I googled "how to stop drinking." I found a twelve-step program. It had a quiz:

"If you answer 'yes' to four of the following twelve questions, you might have a problem with alcohol."

I answered "yes" to eleven.

Welp.

I didn't want to admit I was sick. But I knew I couldn't keep this up. I'd lose everything—or die.

I called my brother. His wife is in recovery. He'd suspected for years that I had a problem. He didn't judge. He just told me to try quitting for ninety days. "If you can't, you'll know," he said.

It seemed reasonable. I'd white-knuckle through it. I'd prove myself wrong. I had willpower. I'd do it for my family.

He also told me to go to an AA meeting—just in case. Warned me that if I went back to drinking, it might get worse.

He was right.

So... My day count began.

# White Knuckles and a Broken Parachute

The first week or so was a breeze.

I didn't have a problem at all. I avoided most drinking situations and doubled down on exercise to keep my energy up. I told myself I was fine. Strong. In control.

But even though I wasn't drinking, my moods were still erratic.

I'd guzzle energy drinks in the morning, pop a couple of Benadryl to unwind, and drink NyQuil at night just to fall asleep.

As long as I wasn't *drinking*, I told myself, I was keeping my end of the bargain, right?

But in reality, I was still chasing numb.

The drinking was just a symptom of all the other shit rolling around in my head—the pain, the sadness, the anxiety, the depression, the pressure. It was all still there.

Only now, there was nothing to distract me.

No bottle to blur the edges. No smoke to soften the blow.

It was all too much, all at once.

As much as drinking and drugs had brought me to my knees, they were also saving me.

My armor. My protection. My safety net.

Without them, I was vulnerable—like a country mouse cornered by a Burmese python.

Then it got tougher. Much tougher.

With every party and every social situation, more and more people asked:

"Why aren't you drinking?"

"Quit again? Why this time?"

"Come on—just have one."

And I didn't have a good answer.

Not one I felt like saying out loud, anyway.

It all started to feel less like a challenge and more like torture.

Dinners out became minefields of anxiety.

I was having panic attacks.

I hated the questions. I hated not knowing what to say. I hated envying people for being able to drink like it was nothing.

Every place I went made me crave a drink.

The Buddha said suffering arises from craving. Dude was right.

I was definitely craving.

And I was absolutely suffering.

The only way I can describe it?

It's like getting bitten by a werewolf and starting to change—but getting stuck halfway through.

Claws half-pierced through your fingertips.

Spine half-curled.

Legs half-hyperextended and broken backward.

The whole fucking lot of it.

That's what I felt like.

Just... trapped.

The jumping-off point.

Not being able to imagine a life without alcohol—

but knowing, deep down, you can't live with it anymore.

Fucking awful.

I was second-guessing my decision every day.

Why would I want to quit if this is how I was gonna feel?

*What's the point?*

I kept trying to figure out how many days it had been.

I didn't track it properly and exaggerated the time—not exactly lying, but maybe omitting.

I was protecting my streak.

That's what I told myself.

Without my medicine—because that's what alcohol and drugs were —I wasn't pleasant to be around.

Still pretending to be fine on the outside, but at home I was restless, irritable, and discontented.

I didn't want to do anything but go to sleep and somehow wake up on day ninety.

We had a family vacation planned in February with some friends.

I realized ninety days would be up right around the time of that trip.

And suddenly, that became the light at the end of the tunnel.

*Make it to vacation.*

*Prove your point.*

*Party on the beach.*

*Shut everyone the fuck up.*

*Eyes on the prize.*

*You can do this.*

I couldn't.

I made it to New Year's Eve... and cracked.

I was nervous the entire week leading up to it.

We were hosting that night. Everyone knew I wasn't drinking.

And I hated that.

I hated being the odd man out—watching everyone else loosen up while I sat there sipping a club soda with a twist of *fuck my life*.

I still made sure we had enough alcohol.

Beer, vodka, gin, bottles of champagne for midnight.

And for me? A six-pack of Rockstar energy drinks.

Because I wasn't drinking, but I'd still throw back 100 ounces of liquid heart attack.

It didn't take much.

Fifteen minutes into the party, I cracked open a bottle of Grey Goose and mixed it with the Rockstar.

I felt horribly guilty and weak...

for about fifteen minutes.

And then the alcohol took care of the rest.

I was off to the races.

Just like that.

Buzzed. Wasted. Free.

It felt amazing to feel that lightness again.

I was back off the wagon—and I could finally exhale.

Only I didn't.

Because, just like my brother said... the drinking got worse.

I didn't have the tools to handle life without alcohol.

Sure, I could run a business, go grocery shopping, take my kid to her soccer game.

But the *inside stuff*—the stuff that makes you tick—that was rotting. Dying on the vine.

I hadn't faced a problem *without* alcohol *ever*.

That was my answer.

That was my language.

I didn't know how to function without it.

Trying to quit for those ninety days was like jumping out of an airplane without a parachute.

Not recommended.

Never ends well.

Things went to shit quickly.

I hadn't fixed anything.

Not my marriage.

Not my moods.

Not the hole inside me.

I just pressed pause.

My relationship with Ronni deteriorated fast.

We started to resent each other. Fought constantly. Slept apart.

Our daughter asked us if we were getting divorced.

By that point, Ronni had witnessed multiple bottoms.

And she couldn't understand how any human being—let alone the man she chose to build a life with—could keep doing the same insane things over and over, when it was clearly killing him.

She must've felt like she was living with a stranger.

Never knowing which version of me was going to walk through the door.

The guilt.

The stress.

The shame.

It was all crushing me.

The beers at work.

The drinks on the train.

It wasn't a bad stretch anymore—it was my baseline.

I couldn't stand to look at myself in the mirror.

I thought about checking into a psych ward just so I could rest.

So I could stop pretending.

So I could escape.

I wanted to be free of responsibility.

I couldn't focus.

I just wanted to be numb.

I hated myself.

And I was terrified of what I was becoming.

I started thinking about death.

Not actively planning it—but... wondering.

What would it be like to just disappear?

Would my family be better off without me?

Would my daughters ever understand?

I felt like a ghost in my own life.

*And I wasn't done falling yet.*

# Train Diaries: Old Man, Look at My Life
## Written March 10, 2010

I t's Friday evening.

The train hums toward home, and I'm trying—like always—to unwind.

I get worked up during the day.

Sometimes the stress feels so heavy it bends the wires inside my brain.

I keep the tension inside.

I always have.

My insides are older than my outsides.

I need the train ride home.

I need the solitude.

Fifty-three minutes to clear out the cobwebs doesn't sound like much,

but sometimes it's the only thing that keeps me from collapsing on my own doorstep.

*I build my cocoon quickly.*

*Each thread spun from the noises of the train—*

*the wheels shrieking against the rails,*

*the dull murmur of tired conversations,*

*the soft clack of laptops snapping shut.*

*It's a symphony.*

*It's human Gatorade.*

*Soul quenching.*

*We're all here for the same reason.*

*Trying to be whole again before we step back into the lives waiting for us.*

*But God, I'm tired.*

*So tired all the time.*

*I notice an old man sitting a few seats down.*

*He's humming a tune under his breath.*

*I can't catch the melody, but it's low and steady—*

*like a thousand bumblebees trapped under glass.*

*Other people look annoyed.*

*He's breaking their fragile commuter concentration.*

*Not me.*

*His humming pulls me inward.*

*It's comforting.*

*Warm.*

*Human.*

*I start to wonder if he's me, forty years from now.*

*So many years spent riding this same train.*

*I wonder if he still has someone waiting for him at home.*

*I wonder if he still gets hugs—*

*the kind with the running start,*

*the kind that end with a thud on the floor and laughing breathless in the hallway.*

*I wonder if his kids still call.*

*I wonder if he still feels like he belongs somewhere when he steps off the train.*

*My heart aches for him.*

*And for myself.*

*I want to share my hugs with him.*

*The whole bundle of them.*

*The ones I'm racing toward right now.*

*The ones that, some nights, feel like the only thing keeping me moving forward at all.*

*He hums.*

*I listen.*

*And for a little while,*

*the train feels less like a cage*

*and more like a place where maybe—just maybe—*

*you can still find a little music in the noise.*

# The Last Storm

My wife and I had started marriage counseling.

It was my idea. A Hail Mary.

I wanted to show her I was serious about changing—to prove I still cared.

But the truth is, in my head, it wasn't about my drinking or my mental health.

I thought maybe *she* was the problem.

If she just understood how hard it was to be me... maybe she'd cut me some slack.

Let me be. Ease up. Stop asking so much.

I told myself I was drinking because of how bad things were at home. Not the other way around.

I never saw my part in anything.

Every time I fucked up and she got angry, I resented her.

I didn't think, *Of course she's angry.*

I thought, *You'd drink too if you had the pressure I have—work, the blog, all these people counting on me, Magnus blowing up the office every day.*

I was blind.

Selfish.

So far up my own ass I couldn't see the damage I was doing.

Looking back, I'm disgusted by how unaware I was.

How convinced I was that I was the victim.

Ronni didn't want to go to counseling, but she agreed—reluctantly.

Maybe she already knew it wouldn't work.

That I wasn't capable of being honest.

That I'd just blame everyone else, like I always did.

I couldn't even be honest with the guy in the mirror, let alone a therapist.

But I was a master manipulator.

I could paint myself as the good guy. The great dad. The perfect husband. The guy who *deserved* a drink after work.

*I run a business. I have clients. Of course I come home late. It's not just me.*

We went every week.

We spun in circles.

And I kept drinking.

Even after the misplaced car.

The Penn Station bathroom floor.

Even after falling short of the ninety days, I still thought I could manage it.

It was late February 2010.

We had just gotten back from our family vacation, and somehow I'd managed to avoid any disasters—which felt like a miracle at the time.

That Thursday, the city and Long Island were bracing for a snowstorm. A real one.

They were calling for nearly two feet. The kind of storm that shuts everything down.

I had plans to stop at a bar after work.

One of our longtime employees was leaving, and I wanted to buy the first round. A quick sendoff. I was the boss—I felt obligated to show my face.

Ronni asked me not to go.

She was worried they'd stop the trains if the storm hit hard—that I'd get stranded.

She didn't want me dying in the snow like Jack Nicholson in *The Shining*.

It wasn't a stretch.

I told her I'd only have one. Maybe two.

I said I didn't even *want* to drink—which, at that moment, was true.

I told her I'd be on the 7:19 train. Home by 8:30.

She wasn't thrilled, but she agreed.

The bar was literally down the block.

We got there around 5:30.

Nice and early.

I bought the first round. Opened a tab. Told my bookkeeper to keep it open for a few rounds after I left—because I was a *good guy* like that.

One beer turned into one shot.

The shot didn't hit hard, so I ordered a second beer to nurse before heading out.

It had started snowing, but nothing serious. I texted Ronni to say I was leaving by 6:45.

At 6:30, someone ordered another round of shots.

Tequila this time. I threw it back, hit the bathroom, came out, and started saying my goodbyes.

I meant it.

I really was going to leave.

I put on my jacket and walked toward the door.

And then—

One of my good friends walked in.

Total coincidence. He had a couple work buddies with him.

Big hug. Big laugh.

"Where you going?" he asked.

"I gotta catch the train before the snow gets bad," I said. "I promised Ronni. I already texted her I was on my way."

He asked me to stay for one drink.

I said no.

He asked again.

I said no again.

Then he reached into his pocket and handed me something—low key.

A small bag of coke.

I wasn't a big coke guy. But if it was there, I was doing it.

He told me, "Just hit the bathroom with me. Quick line for the road."

I figured, *What the hell. It'll wear off by the time I get home.*

Ronni would never know.

So we went in.

One line.

Then another.

Then another.

And just like that—it happened.

That switch.

That flick.

That familiar moment where all bets are off and *nothing matters anymore.*

Not Ronni.

Not the snow.

Not the train.

Not the promise.

I walked out and grabbed another beer. Another shot.

My phone started vibrating.

It was 7:30.

Ronni was calling. Probably checking if I made the train.

I didn't answer.

I figured I'd catch the next one.

Blame it on delays.

Call her from the platform.

Another beer.

Another line.

Another missed call.

And another.

And another.

Next thing I knew, it was 11 p.m.

My coworkers were long gone.

It was just me, my friend, and his people.

I looked at my phone.

At the call log.

At the time.

And I felt that sick, sinking weight in my stomach.

The one that always showed up too late.

I threw on my coat and walked outside.

The streets were empty.

There was half a foot of snow on the ground.

I could barely see ten feet in front of me.

I remember so vividly—

Walking uptown on 7th Ave.

Looking up at the streetlights.

Watching the snow fall in front of them.

Just white.

Just nothing.

I was drunk.

Wired.

Alone.

Trying to get to a train that might never come.

*What the fuck is wrong with you?*

*Why are you so fucking stupid?*

*How did you get here again?*

Penn Station was half-empty.

The last train of the night wasn't until after midnight.

I sat down.

Tried to think of what I could possibly say to Ronni.

I was ashamed.

Defeated.

Done.

Somehow... I knew I was done.

I got home after 1 a.m.

The whole neighborhood was blanketed in white.

I walked in quietly.

Tried not to wake anyone.

Got undressed and slipped into bed.

Ronni might've been asleep.

Or pretending to be.

There was nothing left to say.

I didn't know what was going to happen the next day.

I just knew the jig was up.

Something had to give.

I swear on my kids' lives, I never intended to have more than one beer that night.

I meant it.

I really did.

But that's the thing about addiction. It decides for you.

I didn't choose alcohol and coke that night.

They chose me.

They always chose me.

# Better

Ronni and I didn't really talk about the blizzard incident. I guess she was done talking. Talking about my fuckups and broken promises? She might as well have been talking to a deaf Chihuahua.

But we kept going to marriage counseling. The sessions were uncomfortable. Something had shifted that night during the storm. I don't know if I'd call it a moment of clarity—more like a moment of: *Hey, dumbass, you're fucking it all up. Everything. And you've run out of chances.*

My life was the emotional equivalent of a baby calf crossing a crocodile swamp at the same time every day. Sooner or later, it was gonna get torn apart.

A day or two before our next session, I asked Ronni if I could go alone. I didn't know what I was going to say—I just knew I needed to *tell* someone. I could've told *her*, the one person who cared about me the most. But I couldn't. Saying it out loud would mean she'd *know* I was broken. Not just a screwup who couldn't control his drinking, but actually broken. Maybe unfixable.

And if I was unfixable... why would she stay?

It'd be like riding a bike with two flat tires. It would be much easier to just get new tires. I was past the point of patching or pumping. And it killed me to think she might finally realize that—and trade me in for someone shinier, faster, better.

I felt like I was coming apart at the seams. Like a cheap sweater from the Salvation Army. Completely and utterly demoralized.

She agreed. I think she welcomed the break from hearing the same $250-an-hour bullshit week after week.

When I got to the appointment, I stalled—small talk, the weather, my blog, how annoying work was. All of it a weak attempt to delay the inevitable. But she just kept looking at me like she was waiting for the end of a filibuster.

I opened my mouth three times before anything came out.

Part of me wanted to lie again. Just a light version of the truth. Something honest-*ish* that would pass inspection but keep the rest locked away. But the other part—the one that couldn't breathe anymore—took over.

And then—I said it.

For the first time in my life, I told someone the truth.

I told her how much I relied on alcohol. The pills. Energy drinks. How miserable I was. How long the depression had been living in me. The anxiety, going all the way back to childhood. I told her I'd been thinking about disappearing—just *not being here* anymore. And how I didn't think anything could fix me.

The rot inside me cracked open, and it all came pouring out—like a busted fire hydrant.

She just listened. And holy shit, I needed that. No questions. No yelling. No judgment. No "Have you tried yoga?" Just quiet, steady listening.

I don't know when I started crying, but by the time I stopped, my face was soaked and snot was dripping from my nose. The weight that lifted... like a ten-ton piano finally hit the ground, and for once, I wasn't standing beneath it.

She told me to breathe. To feel it. Not to be afraid to let it all go.

Then she asked how I felt.

And I didn't know how to answer. I'd been asked that question a million times, and the answer was always the same. *I'm fine.* I'd never felt anything long enough to even *process* it. I'd always plugged the leak with booze or pills before the words could get out. But I paused, caught my breath, and said the only thing that came to mind:

"Better."

That was it. Just... better. It might not sound like much, but *better* was huge. It was new. It was a start. The first pour of cement into a foundation I'd never had.

She asked if I'd be open to medication—for depression, for anxiety. I pushed back. *Side effects. Cost. Blah blah blah.*

But the truth? I was ashamed.

I felt like a failure. Like I should be able to fix myself. That needing help made me weak. Broken.

And then she hit me with something that cracked my whole story wide open:

"People medicate when they're sick."

I wasn't weak. I wasn't broken. I was sick.

She looked at me and said, "If you had diabetes, would you take insulin? If you had a treatable cancer, would you say no to chemo?"

"It's the same thing," she said. "There's nothing to be ashamed of. You're not alone."

That last line hit me in the chest. *You're not alone.* I had people around me. People that cared. Ronni. My daughters. Three thousand Facebook friends for Christ's sake. But I'd never felt more alone. Because I thought my pain was unique.

And then she dropped the truth bomb:

"What's the difference between the medicine a doctor would prescribe you and the self-medicating you've been doing for twenty-five years?"

I had no answer.

That night, she gave me the name of a psychiatrist. Asked me if I'd meet with him. Just to talk. She said he might be able to help me understand what was going on in my head—and why I'd been drowning for so long.

She said my mental health was likely the root of everything. The drinking, the drugs—just symptoms. But if I was as determined to get better as I had been to self-destruct, I might just have a shot.

Before I left, she suggested one more thing—not a command, just a nudge:

"Would you consider going to an AA meeting?"

What did that even mean? Where would I find one? How many would I need to go to? Was I really *that* bad? But honestly... I was desperate. So I nodded. I said I'd think about it. But I knew I didn't have time to think. I'd wasted enough of that.

I thanked her and I left.

And I felt different.

*Better.*

I got in the car and something told me to call my dad. We hadn't spoken in months. He hadn't seen his grandkids in over a year. I'd convinced myself it didn't bother me—but it had. Lately, it'd been leaking into my dreams.

So I called him from the car.

We talked about nothing, like we usually did. Then he asked how I was. This time I actually told him. I really told him.

I told him I wasn't okay. That I was angry. That I was hurt. That I felt like an afterthought. That he'd cheated me out of so much, whether he realized it or not.

And he told me he hadn't known I felt that way. That I drank that way. And that he was sorry. And I believed him.

I said it'd be nice to see him. For him to see his granddaughters. And he agreed. He said he'd book a flight that night.

We hung up.

It was the most honest, meaningful conversation I'd ever had with my dad.

And again... I felt *better*.

The next day, I had tickets to the Rangers–Islanders game. I was meeting one of the guys. Normally, that meant getting hammered. Natural habitat. Home ice advantage.

I almost didn't go. I didn't trust myself. But I went anyway.

We met at Charley O's, like always. He already had a beer waiting for me. Normally I'd grab it without thinking.

This time, I thought about *everything*.

I took a sip—and it tasted like poison.

Not metaphorical poison. *Real* poison. Because it wouldn't make me feel better. Not the kind of better I wanted now. The better I needed. The better I'd tasted the night before.

I put the beer down. Half full.

We went to the game. The Rangers won. I remembered the whole damn thing.

I got on the train I said I'd be on.

That was my last drink.

March 24, 2010.

No crash. No sirens. No jail cell or hospital bed.

Just done.

I still had one more thing to do. That could wait until the next day.

I went to bed.

And it was the best sleep I'd had in years.

And for the first time in a long time...

I actually looked forward to waking up.

# One Last Breath

Y ou never know when your life is about to change.

Not the big, obvious changes—weddings, babies, funerals.

I'm talking about the quiet pivots.

The small, unsuspecting moments that don't look like anything until you look back and realize: *That was it.*

*That was the day.*

For me, it was a Thursday. A little warm for March.

My wife had already left for work. I got the girls ready and dropped them off at school.

No hangover. No shame spiral. Just... clarity.

A strange kind of calm—like waking from a nightmare you can't remember, but still feeling grateful it's over.

The change of seasons always came with false promises.

Winter was always heavier. More depression. More dread.

And every year, I convinced myself spring would fix it.

That sunshine and flowers could undo years of damage.

Maybe for a minute. Then the flicker would blow out again.

But something was different that day.

It's hard to explain. Maybe it was the air. The way the sunlight hit the street. Or maybe it was just me.

Perspective is powerful. It can flip the same scene from hell to holy.

A rainy day can feel like a threat or a reset, depending on how you're wired.

I'd spent years waking up on the wrong side of the bed—like I was sleeping at the far end of a seesaw.

But that morning? It felt like the right side. For the first time in a long time.

After I dropped the kids off, I headed to the train.

A song came on the radio—"One Last Breath" by Creed.

I'd heard it before, but never really *heard* it.

Creed was basically the Nickelback of Christian rock. Everyone hated them. At least Nickelback was Canadian—hard to hate Canada.

Normally, I'd change the station.

But not that day. That day, I listened.

Halfway through the song, I started crying.

It hit me like a wave. The lyrics, the melody, the ache in his voice—

It was like the song had been hiding in the background of my life, waiting for this moment.

One line hooked straight into my chest:

*"Hold me now, I'm six feet from the edge..."*

It wrecked me.

It was hopeful and haunting at the same time.

It became the only song I listened to that day.

On repeat.

Like it was the soundtrack to the first scene of a new life.

I walked into Emerald and the usual chaos was already in full swing.

People popping their heads in: "Got a sec?"

Magnus pacing like a mongoose on Adderall.

I passed the beer tap in the kitchen a dozen times and didn't blink.

I accidentally kicked an old bottle of Grey Goose under my desk—something I'd stashed months ago.

I nudged it back out of sight.

Creed kept playing. Like white noise. Like armor.

At some point, I remembered what the therapist said—

*Maybe try an AA meeting.*

I kept putting it off. Next week. After the weekend.

But my best thinking had gotten me here—and it wasn't working.

So I googled "AA meetings in NYC."

Hundreds popped up. I figured none would be close.

But there it was—8 p.m. Just a few blocks away.

At 7:30, I packed up and walked over.

I couldn't find the place at first. That creeping sense of defeat kicked in—

*Of course. The one thing that might help is just out of reach.*

I called the number from the site. A woman picked up. She sounded warm.

I told her the name of the meeting and my location.

She said, "You see a big group of kids smoking outside a church?"

I looked up. "Yeah."

She said, "That's your meeting, honey."

I walked through a huge black gate.

The church was set back from the street—dimly lit, wide stone stairs, a thick wooden door that looked like it belonged in Middle Earth, not Manhattan.

For a second, I wondered if I was at the right place or about to break bread with a Hobbit.

Everyone greeted me on the way in.

Smiles. Nods. "Hey, man, glad you're here."

The room was packed—more than a hundred people. Most of them looked like they could still be in college.

It felt like I'd stumbled into a Blink-182 concert.

The lighting was harsh. Metal folding chairs lined the room like punishment for your coccyx.

It was loud. Laughing. Joking. Smiling.

I wasn't sure what they were smiling about—but it felt real. I wondered what I was missing.

I found a seat in the back, on the aisle.

An escape route.

Kept my head down.

Started wondering if I belonged here at all.

Then a young woman—who looked like she'd just graduated from middle school—banged a gavel and called the room to order.

She introduced herself as an alcoholic. The room responded in unison.

It felt a little culty. Like an improv class where everything's an inside joke.

And then she said something I'll never forget:

"Is there anyone here for their first AA meeting?

We don't ask to embarrass you—

but so we can get to know you."

She paused.

I hesitated. My pulse spiked. My face flushed.

And before I could stop myself—my hand went up.

She pointed. "Right there. What's your name?"

The words came out slow. Like I was speaking underwater.

"My name is Jason," I said, "and this is my first meeting."

The room erupted. Cheering. Applause.

I'd never been clapped for just for *showing up* before.

It overwhelmed me.

All I could do was drop my head in my hands and cry.

I cried because I was broken.

Because I was tired.

Because I didn't want to die—but didn't know how to live.

I cried for every promise I'd broken. Every moment I'd missed.

For every time I made the people I loved feel like they didn't matter.

But mostly I cried because I wasn't alone.

People reached out. Hands on my shoulder.

One guy leaned in and whispered, "We've got you, man."

Another passed me a box of tissues.

No one made it weird. No one asked me to stop.

They just let me be.

And for the first time in a long time—I let myself be.

It felt like the price of admission was pain. Regret. Sadness.

And my pockets were full.

I don't remember the rest of the meeting.

The speaker, the shares, the announcements—blurred.

I just remember feeling the weight start to lift.

Not all at once. Not like a miracle.

More like someone loosening a noose I'd been strangled by for years.

When the meeting ended, I made for the exit.

But I didn't get far.

A circle of guys closed in—like a wall of kindness.

They hugged me. Introduced themselves.

Handed me scraps of paper with their names and phone numbers.

Encouragement written in ballpoint ink.

One guy hung back as the crowd thinned. Older. Closer to my age.

Kind eyes. No hard sell.

"Hey," he said. "I'm Eric."

We talked for a minute. No pressure. No lecture.

Just, *How you doing?*

Then he asked for my number.

I hesitated.

But I gave it to him.

"I'll call you tomorrow," he said. "It was really good to meet you."

And for some reason—I believed him.

I walked out into the night air and just stood there.

Breathing.

Watching the wind stir the trees like it was shaking something loose in me—

Something I thought was gone.

Something human.

I took the long walk back to Penn Station with "One Last Breath" in my ears.

I didn't cry.

I just listened.

Noticed things—

The hum of the city.

The flicker of streetlights.

The way the world kept turning—

like maybe I had a place in it.

I didn't feel like a ghost anymore.

I didn't know what came next.

But I knew this much:

I wasn't six feet from the edge.

Not tonight.

And if this was my one last breath?

I was finally ready to use it—

To live.

# Epilogue

This isn't the end of my story. It's kind of just the beginning.

Call it whatever you want—second chance? I've had way more than two. Ask my wife—she gave me at least a hundred.

Starting over? Fuck that. I don't want to do it all over again. That would be a nightmare.

Nine lives? *Oy vey.* I don't have the stamina. And I'm way more of a dog person anyway.

It's more of a new beginning vibe.

Yeah, that feels right.

And that's the track I've been on for over fifteen years now: better. One day at a time.

I'm not saying there aren't days I don't feel worse. But that perspective thing? It's always accessible.

Some days are just harder.

My old sponsor used to say, "It's okay to get in a rut, kid. Just don't decorate it."

I'll admit—I've definitely taken a few trips to HomeGoods.

But now? I keep the receipts.

Not many people get two beginnings.

Not many people *need* them, I guess.

But I did.

One of the reasons I wrote this book was to look at my life in chapters—literally and figuratively.

Because if I don't, it all feels like one long, chaotic run-on sentence.

And I've lived the no-chapter version.

Hollowed out. Survival-only. Always bracing for the next hit.

Now? I want structure. I want reflection.

I want to know where one thing ends and something better begins.

Because if you can't finish a chapter, you can't move on.

And *not* moving on? That's been the root of most of my suffering.

The self-pity. The shame. The sabotage.

All of it? Chapters.

And the good stuff? Also chapters.

One book? Maybe.

But writing it all down—breaking it into pages and arcs and sections—helped me make sense of it.

Helped me accept it.

Sometimes overanalyze it.

But mostly? It helped me move on.

Today, my life is better.

Ronni and I have been together for over thirty years.

That's more than two hundred dog years.

And if you ask her, she'll probably say she feels like the world's oldest Poodle.

But we've built a beautiful life.

Our girls? Full-blown, real, adult humans. Strong, curious, and kind.

My mom? We hang out almost every week. We text. We're good.

She knows who I am now and how hard I've worked to get here.

She knows it wasn't her fault—because she's done the work, too.

Same with my dad. We've come a long way.

Things that used to feel impossible to say are now just... part of the conversation.

Not perfect—but real. And that matters.

Mom, my dad—even Damon—they all did the best they could with what they had.

Empathy is a gift. Hell, it's a superpower.

And unlike Superman, I don't think you're born with it.

It's more of a Dark Knight thing. You earn it.

You, me, all of us—we've got origin stories.

I guess this book was mine.

Would it make a good movie? Probably not.

But if someone did, I'd want Danny Bonaduce to play me as a kid.

As an adult? Toss-up between Ryan Gosling and Jason Biggs. Flip a coin.

That career that kicked the living shit out of me? I'm grateful for it.

Every person, every office, every meltdown—I learned something.

From Gary. Lillian. Courtney. Magnus.

Even that sleazy prick who called Ronni my "trophy wife"—which, by the way, *facts*—taught me something.

It took me a decade of sobriety *and* a full-blown global pandemic to realize I didn't get sober just to be miserable.

Now I have a job that fills my bucket.

It gives me purpose—and the privilege of giving back what was freely given to me.

I work as a peer advocate, using my lived experience to help others find their way forward.

I go into jails, schools, rehabs, community coalitions—I even started a recovery meeting just for dads.

I don't show up with advice.

I show up to listen, to connect, and to remind people they're not alone.

Recovering out loud isn't for everyone.

It wasn't for me—not until I changed careers.

But I didn't go through all that pain just to keep it to myself.

It had to count for something.

That's what led me to start Sober Not Subtle—a platform to amplify the voices of people in recovery, families affected by addiction, behavioral health professionals, and sober allies.

It exists to fight stigma.

To normalize the conversation around mental health and substance use disorder.

Because these stories matter—and they deserve to be heard.

The money? Not so much.

But Ronni gets to be my sugar momma now—and honestly, that's hot as fuck.

I've experienced real loss in sobriety. Family. Friends.

I lost four of them—two in a single day once.

I cried my eyes out.

And I still think about them all the time.

But I'm grateful I was there.

Present. Sober. Feeling it.

At five years sober, I thought I was losing my mind.

At thirteen, I almost checked myself into a psych ward.

But not once did I drink. Not once did I numb.

Did I want to?

Absolutely.

I'm human.

But now I know there's nothing so painful I can't get through by asking for help.

So if there's one thing you take from this—let it be this:

Ask for help.

Everyone needs it.

But sometimes the phone—or hologram projector, or whatever tech we've got by the time you read this—feels like it weighs a thousand pounds.

Use a spotter.

Reach out.

We lose too many people to silence.

And if you're someone who thinks they need to escape—

through alcohol, or food, or porn, or pills, or gambling, or whatever your thing is—

there are other ways.

I promise you.

Like those kids outside the church-slash-Blink-182 concert told me in my darkest moment:

*We got you.*

So just for one second, give in to that part of you that *knows*—deep down—you deserve better.

*Better* is the only start you need.

So take a breath.

Turn that frown upside down.

Give perspective a chance.

*Believe me. It gets better.*


P.S. That dad blog I used to write?

About a week after I got sober, I sat my ass down on the train and finally found the courage to write something.

Turned out, it was the most honest thing I'd ever written.

I still read it sometimes—to remember what it felt like to have a new beginning.

I guess that's my mic drop... before I close this dusty old laptop and go play *Fortnite* with my buddies.

I hope it helps someone.


## Train Diaries: Concrete. Brick. Mortar. Repeat.

*Written April 4, 2010*


*The bathroom in my bedroom has a window right behind the toilet.*

*This morning I was peeing and staring out into the yard.*

*I spotted a bumble bee crawling across the roof.*

*Spring.*

*The seasons can signify many things. I suppose it depends on who you are.*

*For most, I would imagine they bring hope, change or inspiration. Perhaps all three.*

*But not me.*

*I don't think I've ever needed the Spring as much as I do now.*

*The sun is like an awakening of sorts. Its bright light can change everything in an instant. There's something about the warmth, the light, the smell of green.*

*So I've heard.*

*I've needed a change for quite some time. So long, that it's hard for me to explain. It might be easier for me to speak in metaphors. I'm not quite ready to talk about all of this. But I need to let it go.*

*Suppose for the past 30 years you had been walking in the cold, gray Winter. What if you'd watched countless seasons come and go but the Spring had always eluded you?*

*What if most days seemed as if they were filled with dark clouds and rain? So much rain. Imagine the Winter never left and Spring never came.*

*What would you do?*

*What could you do?*

*I can feel the Spring today. I can feel it for the first time in a long time.*

*For 30 years, I've carried a huge burden with me. I've harbored a lot of anger. I've tucked years of resentment so far down in my soul that I had forgotten it was even there.*

*But it was there.*

*Hardened.*

*Rotten.*

*Resentment has been the foundation for a wall I've built so high that I couldn't even see over the top of it.*

*Concrete. Brick. Mortar. Repeat.*

*Mom, Dad, Wife, Children, Friends.*

*All on the other side.*

*My parents got divorced when I was 9. I remember the night they told me. I think that was the beginning. That night I locked the door to my heart and threw away the key. I wouldn't ever talk about it again. I wouldn't bother anyone. I wouldn't listen to anyone.*

*I wouldn't do anything.*

*I spent the last 30 years avoiding contact. I did whatever it took to stay at an arm's length away. I wouldn't let anyone get even remotely close for more than a moment. I was afraid.*

*What could a 9-year-old boy be so afraid of? What could a 39-year-old man, with a job, a house and a family, be so scared of?*

*It's simple.*

*I was afraid of being disappointed. I was afraid of being let down. I was afraid that it would happen all over again.*

*I was angry at my father for leaving and I resented my mother for letting him go.*

*It's amazing what the mind will do to preserve one's own sanity. Or maybe it's just tragic.*

*I would take care of myself. I would wedge anything and everything between me and anyone who wanted a piece of me.*

*I would use alcohol, pills, food, whatever it took to numb the pain. I would self medicate for 30 years. I even used this blog. Especially this blog. It's the perfect form of contact. It's indirect. It's not real. It's safe because you can't get too close to me...*

*Until now.*

*I'm changing.*

*I can feel it. For the first time, I'm starting to let go. I'm turning over the reins to a power greater than myself. I'm letting the resentment go and I'm inviting the ones that I love back in. I'm putting trust in faith. I'm having faith in trust.*

*These past few weeks have been hard. But not nearly as hard as all of the weeks prior. Over a thousand weeks gone for good. So much wasted time.*

*I must do this. I will not waste any more time.*

*I've taken some big steps to make things right. Things I'm not ready to talk about right now. Not here.*

*Today I felt the Spring for the first time in a long time. It's never felt so fucking good...*

# Acknowledgments

Writing this book would not have been possible without a consistent drip of cold brew and a few places that let me loiter—physically and mentally. Thank you to Catskills Coffee Lodge for the caffeine, the kindness, and the beautiful, inspiring scenery that helped clear my head and fill the page. And to Soul Brew Long Island, thank you for the great coffee, the good vibes, and for letting me take my headshots there—proof that your vibe really does attract your tribe. Big love to Jay the chef for serving up the best cheese biscuit on the planet. That thing deserves its own book.

Huge thanks to Michael McConnell for jumping into this project with me and installing some much-needed guardrails. You showed me that editing is about so much more than grammar—it's about finding clarity, truth, and rhythm. Every page is better because of your touch.

To my publisher and tireless cheerleader, Amy Liz Harrison—thank you for your guidance, reassurance, and coaching. You reminded me that even at fifty-four, I still have so much to learn. And that's not only okay—it's the whole point.

To my little brother, who might just be the funniest person alive, thank you for always making me laugh and for reminding me that I have nothing to worry about because, according to you, no one's going to read this book anyway. Love you, dude.

To Kim Grabina-Como, who had possibly the tallest task of all: photographing this tired old face and somehow turning it into something worthy of the back of a book cover. You're very brave—and incredibly talented. Thank you.

To Agata Broncel of Bukovero Design—thank you for bringing the cover of this book to life. Your attention to detail, patience, and creative instinct helped set the tone and capture the emotion behind every page. You nailed it.

To my dad—for always telling me you're proud of me, even though I'm a grown-ass adult. It's still nice to hear those words. They land every time.

To "Ray" and "Matt"—I still can't believe you're gone. I'm sure wherever you are, Ray's buying someone a beer, quoting *The Godfather*, and ranting about the state of the world, while Matt's helping an old lady cross the street and making her smile. I think about you guys every day.

To every single person who's walked with me on this journey—family, friends, and even the ones who weren't so kind—thank you. I probably learned just as much from the hard lessons as I did from the good ones.

To Bill W. and Dr. Bob: thank you for the roadmap back to sanity. Without it, I'd probably be dead—or worse, still drinking and numbing my way through life.

To my new work family—thank you for welcoming me into the world of peer advocacy and for showing me that the skills I used in my old career could also be used to help people heal—and for teaching me that self-care isn't weakness, it's strength.

And finally, to the nine-year-old version of me who took a shitload of shrapnel but somehow kept moving forward: I got it from here.

# About the Author

Jason Mayo is the founder of Sober Not Subtle, a storytelling and advocacy platform focused on breaking the stigma around addiction, recovery, and mental health. He's a Certified Recovery Peer Advocate (CRPA), Certified Addictions Recovery Coach (CARC), and New York Certified Peer Specialist–Provisional (NYCPS-P). He serves as a community outreach coordinator at a local recovery community center, where he facilitates a weekly dads' group, runs sessions at the county jail, trains others in Narcan use, and speaks at schools to share his lived experience with mental health and addiction. He's also an active member of several community action and prevention coalitions.

Jason is a contributing writer for The Sober Curator and previously wrote as a member of the Forbes Business Council, sharing insights on leadership, purpose, and personal growth.

Before entering the behavioral health field, Jason owned and operated award-winning visual effects and animation companies in New York City, partnering with some of the world's top global brands. He's a Twitch Partner and content creator, an avid tattoo collector, a lifelong metalhead, and a proud zombie enthusiast.

He first gained attention in the parenting world as the creator of the dad blog Out-Numbered, which earned national recognition—including BlogHer's Top 100 Voices of the Year and multiple appearances on Babble's Top 50 Dad Bloggers list. In 2013, Working Mother named him one of the "25 Dads Who Rock." He was once selected to host a reality show about misbehaved toddlers—but was ultimately replaced by a show about weight-loss cats. He's since forgiven the cats. Not so much the execs.

He's also the author of two children's books—Do Witches Make Fishes? and The Boy and the Billy Goat—with all proceeds donated to help children impacted by trauma.

Jason got sober in 2010. He lives in New York with his college sweetheart—together for over 30 years—and their two daughters, who keep him humble. In Case of Emergency, Break Childhood is his debut memoir.

facebook.com/sobernotsubtle

instagram.com/sobernotsubtle

bsky.app/profile/sobernotsubtle.bsky.social

youtube.com/@SoberNotSubtle

linkedin.com/company/sober-not-subtle

# Stay Connected

**Thanks for reading.**

If this book meant something to you—or even just made you feel a little less alone—come visit sobernotsubtle.com.

It's a space I created for honest stories about recovery, mental health, and everything in between. You'll find essays, guest posts, resources, and reminders that the mess is worth talking about.

**Because recovery is real. And it's rarely subtle.**

# Publishing Services
# Accreditation

A-TEAM PRESS

Professional publishing services rendered by A-Team Press, LLC
amylizharrison.com/a-teampressauthorpublishingservices

www.ingramcontent.com/pod-product-compliance
Lightning Source LLC
Chambersburg PA
CBHW021705120626
46545CB00004B/1415